Metropolitan sopranos

Ponselle Steber
Milanov Price

with valuable assistance from Clifford Elkin

Discographies compiled by John Hunt

Metropolitan Sopranos
Published by John Hunt.
Designed by Richard Chluparty

reprinted 2009
ISBN 978-1-901395-01-3

CONTENTS

Sole distributors:
Travis & Emery,
17 Cecil Court,
London, WC2N 4EZ,
United Kingdom.
(+44) 20 7 459 2129.
sales@travis-and-emery.com

Published 1997 by John Hunt
Designed by Richard Chlupaty, London

ACKNOWLEDGEMENT

These publications have been made possible by contributions and advance subscriptions from the following:

Masakasu Abe, Chiba
Richard Ames, New Barnet
Stefano Angeloni, Frasso Sabino
Stathis Arfanis, Athens
Yoshihiro Asada, Osaka
Jack Atkinson, Tasmania
Eduardo Chibas, Caracas
Robert Christoforides, Fordingbridge
F. De Vilder, Bussum
Richard Dennis, Greenhithe
John Derry, Newcastle-upon-Tyne
Hans-Peter Ebner, Milan
Henry Fogel, Chicago
Peter Fu, Hong Kong
Nobuo Fukumoto, Hamamatsu
Peter Fulop, Toronto
James Giles, Sidcup
Jens Golumbus, Hamburg
Jean-Pierre Goossens, Luxembourg
Gordon Grant, Seattle
Johann Gratz, Vienna
Michael Harris, London
Tadashi Hasegawa, Nagoya
Naoya Hirabayashi, Tokyo
Donald Hodgman, Riverside CN
Martin Holland, Sale
Bodo Igesz, New York
Richard Igler, Vienna
Shiro Kawai, Tokyo
Andrew Keener, New Malden
Detlef Kissmann, Solingen
Elisabeth Legge-Schwarzkopf DBE, Zürich
John Mallinson, Hurst Green
Carlo Marinelli, Rome
Finn Moeller Larsen, Virum
Philip Moores, Stafford
Bruce Morrison, Gillingham
W. Moyle, Ombersley
Alan Newcombe, Hamburg
Hugh Palmer, Chelmsford
Jim Parsons, Sutton Coldfield
Laurence Pateman, London
James Pearson, Vienna
Johann Christian Petersen, Hamburg
Tully Potter, Billericay
Patrick Russell, Calstock
Yves Saillard, Mollie-Margot
Neville Sumpter, Northolt
Yoshihiko Suzuki, Tokyo
H.A. Van Dijk, Apeldoorn
Mario Vicentini, Cassano Magnago
Hiromitsu Wada, Chiba
Urs Weber, St Gallen
Nigel Wood, London
G. Wright, Romford

METROPOLITAN SOPRANOS

New York's Metropolitan Opera House has in its 115 years probably contributed more to the musical heritage of the United States than any other American institution. It hosted the activities of great operatic reformers like Mahler and Toscanini and witnessed the development of many a legendary singer. And almost all of these singers were captured for the gramophone record, at however late a stage of their careers or under whatever primitive recording conditions. Originally from Europe, the Met's roster of artists eventually came to nurture a host of home-grown talent or of singers from overseas who grew to regard the United States as their home, both for artistic and other reasons.

Rosa Ponselle, of Italian origin but very American upbringing (her art is analysed in a new 1997 study by James Drake published by Amadeus Press), is unquestionably one of the voices of the century in the lyric dramatic sphere. Many commentators have placed her up among the great singers of all time, demanding that her name be put aside before any comparative analysis of others is undertaken. In her prime technically faultless, Ponselle yet deployed her voice with Italianate warmth and genuine passion.

Zinka Milanov, in contrast to Rosa Ponselle, arrived in the United States as an experienced if obscure soprano from Central Europe, but quickly established herself as a Met favourite in her chosen lyric spinto repertoire. An old-fashioned regality suffused both her vocal style and stage deportment. Far from being your modern "thinking" singer Milanov worked by instinct and schooling alone: she considered, for example, that she was "destined" to command roles like Verdi's two Leonoras ("Forza" and "Trovatore") or the two Amelias ("Ballo" and "Boccanegra"). The way in which her voice moulds her contribution to the Council Chamber scene in the latter opera, albeit in a live recording from late in the career, illustrates this to perfection. For linguistic and temperamental reasons, it seems, Milanov did not embrace American light music as Rosa Ponselle did so persuasively before her, or as Eleanor Steber and Leontyne Price were to do later.

Eleanor Steber shares more than her initials with her European contemporary Elisabeth Schwarzkopf. Faultless technique combined with the creamiest phrasing destined her to be a Mozart specialist, but she also embraced prime Italian and German spinto parts. Steber can be heard as the Metropolitan's first Arabella and as Bayreuth's third

American Elsa (after Lilian Nordica and Gertrude Rennyson). For a native American singer in so commanding a position, there must have been at least a slight tinge of regret that Steber's position at the Met during the 1940s and 1950s was gradually eroded (eclipsed it certainly was not) by the arrival of eminent Europeans like Victoria de los Angeles and Lisa Della Casa.

Two particular distinctions single out **Leontyne Price**. Not only was she the first black female American to achieve unconditional fame in the world of opera - in a career which bestrode America and Europe in equal measure - but she was also the American equivalent of a Callas or a Schwarzkopf in regarding her gramophone career as a separate and equally valid adjunct to stage and concert work: apart from her many complete opera recordings, Price also produced, over a period of some 15 years, a series of recital LPs of stunning diversity, penetrating roles from Purcell to Tchaikovsky which she had never essayed in the theatre.

The 3-column layout continues to be used for these discographies, which are arranged alphabetically by composer (apart from some material of a popular nature where a composer could not always be identified). Information in the first column indicates the city where the recording took place, followed now by a precise date wherever possible (day, month, year). Where a recording was spread over a period of time, only the first and last dates are given, but this does not always imply that sessions took place on all intervening days. Second column lists other artists taking part, such as singers, instrumentalists, accompanists or orchestras (the only abbreviations here are the familiar ones for London orchestras: LSO, LPO, RPO). The third column of the discography attempts to list as many catalogue numbers as possible for the main territories and for the principal formats of 78, EP (45), LP and CD (cassette tapes are not normally included). Information may not be complete for all countries and I am always glad to hear from collectors who can add numbers or correct any possible errors. Catalogue numbers which appear on the same line of text, usually separated by "/", often indicate the simultaneous mono and stereo editions of an LP which became customary in the 1950s and 1960s. For example, Victor prefixes LM or RB (mono) may be followed by LSC or SB (stereo), American Columbia ML (mono) by MS (stereo). It should also be borne in mind that some catalogue numbers may be for sets in which the work in question is grouped together with other pieces.

In the case of complete opera recordings, the second column of the discography is headed by an indication of which role the artist takes, and it can be assumed that this remains the same in later recordings of the same opera unless otherwise indicated. Records containing only excerpts from operas or other works are only mentioned in the third column of the discography if they involve the particular singer whose discography is being covered.

Rosa Ponselle
1897-1981

Discography compiled
by John Hunt

To Bill Holland
Sincerely
Rosa Ponselle
as "Norma" 1976

FERMIN ALVAREZ (Died 1898)

La partida

Baltimore 18 October 1954	Chicagov, piano	LP: Victor LM 2047 CD: Romophone 810 222

ANTON ARENSKY (1861-1906)

But lately in dance

New York 18 October 1931	Romani, piano	Unpublished radio broadcast

On wings of dream

New York 19 January 1933		Unpublished radio broadcast
Hollywood 1 November 1939	M.Schmidt, violin Romani, piano Sung in English	Victor 16451 LP: Victor CAL 100/CDN 1006-1007 CD: Nimbus NI 1777/NI 7805 CD: Romophone 810 222 CD: Vocal Archives VA 1120 CD: Legato BIM 701 CD: Minerva MNA 7

JOHANN SEBASTIAN BACH (1685-1750)

Ave Maria, arranged by Gounod

Camden NJ 19 May 1926	M.Schmidt, piano Orchestra Bourdon	Victor 6599 HMV DB 1052 45: Victor WCT 8 LP: Victor LCT 1005 CD: RCA/BMG GD 87810 CD: Nimbus NI 1777/NI 7846 CD: Romophone 810 072
New York 1 January 1927	Orchestra Shilkret	Unpublished radio broadcast Probably Ponselle's radio debut

An earlier Columbia recording of the piece was mentioned in the May 1950 edition of Record Collector

JAMES BARTLETT (1850-1929)

A dream

New York 26 November 1934	Orchestra Kostelanetz	LP: Ed Smith EJS 243 LP: Collectors Limited Edition MDP 012

LUDWIG VAN BEETHOVEN (1770-1827)

In questa tomba oscura

Baltimore 17 October 1954	Chicagov, piano	LP: Victor LM 1889/L 16493 CD: Romophone 810 222

Earlier private recordings of the song, from January 1951 and October 1951, may also survive

VINCENZO BELLINI (1801-1835)

Norma

New York 26 December 1931	Role of Norma Swarthout, Egener, Lauri-Volpi, Pinza Metropolitan Opera Orchestra & Chorus Serafin	Unpublished Met broadcast Only Acts 2 and 3 were broadcast

Norma, excerpt (Casta diva)

New York 11 December 1919	Orchestra Romani	Columbia 49720/68060D/7063M LP: Ember GVC 9 LP: Scala (USA) 803 LP: Pearl GEMM 207 CD: Pearl GEMMCDS 9964 GVC 9 incorrectly dated May 1921
New York 3 December 1928	Orchestra Goossens	Unpublished radio broadcast
Camden NJ 31 December 1928- 30 January 1929	Metropolitan Opera Orchestra & Chorus Setti	Victor 8125 HMV DB 1280 LP: Victor LM 1909/TVM 17202/CBL 100/ CDN 1006-1007/PVM1-9047/ AG 26.41371 CD: RCA/BMG GD 87810 CD: Nimbus NI 1777/NI 7801/NI 7805 CD: Romophone 810 072 CD: Pearl CD 9317 This version includes preceding recitative Sediziose voci!
New York 24 December 1933	Metropolitan Opera Orchestra & Chorus Bodansky	Unpublished radio broadcast

Norma, excerpt (Mira o Norma!)

Camden 30 January 1929	Telva Metropolitan Opera Orchestra Setti	Victor 8110 HMV DB 1276 45: Victor WCT 6 LP: Victor LCT 1004/TVM 17202/CBL 100/ CDN 1006-1007/PVM1-9047/ AG 26.41371 LP: Pearl GEMM 207 CD: Nimbus NI 1777/NI 7805 CD: Romophone 810 072 CD: Metropolitan Opera MET 218 CD: Pearl CD 9317

A private recording of the duet, dated 28 May 1953 with Nuttall, may also survive

HENRY BISHOP (1786-1855)

Home sweet home

New York 16 February 1921	Orchestra Romani	Columbia 49935/68065D/7064M LP: Scala (USA) 851 CD: Pearl GEMMCDS 9964 Pearl incorrectly names composer as Foster
Camden NJ 3 June 1925	Orchestra Pasternack	Victor VB 74 LP: Victor LM 2627/RB 6506 CD: Legato LCD 179 CD: Romophone 810 062
New York 22 January 1933		Unpublished radio broadcast
New York 15 June 1936		Unpublished radio broadcast Performed at Schumann-Heink's birthday celebration; Ponselle also speaks
New York 2 May 1937	Ponselle, piano	LP: Ed Smith EJS 192 LP: Collectors Limited Edition MDP 012 CD: Vocal Archives VA 1120

Unpublished private recording of the song, dated January 1952, may also survive

GEORGES BIZET (1838-1875)

Carmen

New York 1 February 1936	Role of Carmen S.Fisher, Kullmann, Pinza Metropolitan Opera Orchestra & Chorus Hasselmans	Unpublished Met broadcast Excerpts LP: Ed Smith EJS 219/ANNA 1037 Excerpt from this performance also inserted into 28 March 1936 performance (see below)
Boston 28 March 1936	H.Burke, Maison, Pinza Metropolitan Opera Orchestra & Chorus Hasselmans	LP: Ed Smith EJS 116/CAR 1-6 LP: Historical Recording Enterprises HRE 253 CD: Walhall WHL 158 Met performance on tour; CAR 1-6 includes insert from 1 February 1936 performance (see above)
New York 9 January 1937	Bodanya, Rayner, Huehn Metropolitan Opera Orchestra & Chorus Papi	Unpublished Met broadcast
Cleveland 17 April 1937	H.Burke, Maison, Huehn Metropolitan Opera Orchestra & Chorus Papi	LP: Fassett Recording Studio unnumbered Met performance on tour Excerpts LP: Ed Smith EJS 103-104 LP: Metropolitan Opera MET 7 LP: Operatic Archives OPA 10016

Carmen, excerpt (L'amour est un oiseau rebelle)

New York 3 December 1928	Orchestra Goossens	Unpublished radio broadcast
New York 7 December 1930	Orchestra Pasternack	LP: Ed Smith EJS 452 Recording incomplete
New York 25 March 1936	Orchestra Kostelanetz	LP: Ed Smith EJS 190 LP: Collectors Limited Edition MDP 012

Unpublished radio broadcasts dated 22 January 1933, 26 November 1934 and 27 October 1935, as well as a private recording dated 27 October 1951, may also survive

Carmen, excerpt (Près des remparts de Séville)

New York 26 February 1933	Orchestra Kostelanetz	LP: Ed Smith EJS 190 LP: Collectors Limited Edition MDP 012

Unpublished radio broadcasts dated 23 October 1930, 19 February 1933, 11 December 1933, 21 November 1935 and 31 May 1936 may also survive

Carmen, excerpt (Les triangles des sistres)

New York 4 March 1936	Orchestra Kostelanetz	LP: Ed Smith EJS 190 LP: Collectors Limited Edition MDP 012

Unpublished radio broadcasts dated 19 February 1933, 9 April 1934, 8 October 1934 and 27 October 1935 may also survive

Carmen, excerpt (En vain pour éviter)

New York 26 February 1936	Orchestra Kostelanetz	LP: Ed Smith EJS 190 LP: Collectors Limited Edition MDP 012

Unpublished private recordings of the scene, dated 27 October 1951 and 7 December 1953 with Kemp and Nuttall, may also survive

Carmen, excerpt (C'est toi! C'est moi!)

Baltimore 14 December 1952	Kelly Piano accompaniment	Unpublished private recording

Ivan IV, excerpt (Ouvre ton coeur!)

New York 27 September 1936	Orchestra Rapee	LP: Ed Smith EJS 191 LP: Collectors Limited Edition MDP 012

Unpublished radio broadcasts of the aria, dated 22 October 1934 and 18 March 1936 may also survive

Agnus Dei

Baltimore 20 October 1954	Chicagov, piano	CD: Romophone 810 222

JAMES BLAND (1854-1911)

Carry me back to old Virginny

Camden NJ 2 June 1925	Orchestra Pasternack	Victor 6509 HMV DB 872 LP: Pearl GEMM 207 CD: Nimbus NI 1777/NI 7878 CD: Romophone 810 062 Ponselle's first published electrical recording
New York 2 May 1937	Orchestra and Chorus Black	LP: Ed Smith EJS 192
Baltimore 3 April 1953		Unpublished private recording

BLECH

Heine

New York 13 October 1929	Romani, piano	Unpublished radio broadcast

GAETONO BRAGA (1829-1907)

La serenata

New York 18 October 1931	Romani, piano	Unpublished radio broadcast
New York 28 January 1934	Orchestra Shilkret	Unpublished radio broadcast

Further unpublished radio broadcasts of the song, dated 23 October 1930 and 10 December 1934, may also survive

MAY BRAHE (1885-1956)

I passed by your window

New York 27 March 1932		Unpublished radio broadcast

Further unpublished radio broadcasts of the song, dated 12 March 1933 and 11 June 1934, may also survive

JOHANNES BRAHMS (1833-1897)

Von ewiger Liebe

Baltimore 22 November 1953		Unpublished private recording
Baltimore 18 October 1954	Chicagov, piano	LP: Victor LM 1889/L 16493 CD: Romophone 810 222

Wiegenlied

Camden NJ 8 February 1924	Orchestra Bourdon Sung in English	Victor 1002 CD: Romophone 810 062
Camden 8 February 1924	Bourdon, piano Sung in English	Victor unpublished
New York 19 February 1933		Unpublished radio broadcast
New York 15 June 1936		Unpublished radio broadcast Performed at Schumann-Heink's birthday celebration; Ponselle also speaks

JOHANN BRANDL (1835-1913)

Der liebe Augustin, excerpt (Du alter Stephansturm)

New York 11 March 1936	Orchestra Kostelanetz Sung in English in an arrangement by Kreisler	LP: Ed Smith EJS 191 LP: OASI 635 CD: Vocal Archives VA 1120
Cincinatti 25 April 1937	Cincinatti SO Goossens	CD: Eklipse EKRCD 51

Unpublished radio broadcasts dated 23 April 1934 and 17 December 1934 may also survive

HERBERT BREWER (1865-1928)

The fairy pipers

New York 10 April 1930		Unpublished radio broadcast
New York 18 October 1931	Romani, piano	Unpublished radio broadcast

Further unpublished radio broadcasts of the song, dated 25 June 1932 and 17 December 1934, may also survive

BROWN

Flower of the sun

New York 20-27 February 1920	Orchestra Romani	Columbia 49756 This recording was not published

ARTURO BUZZI-PECCIA (1854-1943)

Colombetta

Baltimore 17 October 1954	Chicagov, piano	CD: Romophone 810 222

El morenita

New York 1 April 1936	Orchestra Kostelanetz	LP: Ed Smith EJS 191 LP: Collectors Limited Edition MDP 012

Unpublished radio broadcast dated 31 May 1936 may also survive

ERNEST CHARLES (1895-1984)

When I have sung my songs

New York 18 March 1936	Orchestra Kostelanetz	LP: Ed Smith EJS 191
Hollywood 31 October 1939	Romani, piano	First version Victor VA 68 CD: Nimbus NI 1777/NI 7846 CD: RCA/BMG GD 87810 CD: Romophone 810 222 Second version Victor VA 68 CD: Romophone 810 222

One of the versions of VA 68 is also re-issued on Victor LPs CBL 100/CDN 1006-1007

ERNEST CHAUSSON (1855-1899)

Le temps des lilas (Poème de l'amour et de la mer)

Baltimore 17 October 1954	Chicagov, piano	LP: Victor LM 1889/L 16493 CD: Romophone 810 222

FREDERIC CHOPIN (1810-1849)

Tristesse éternelle, arranged by Litvinne

New York 13 October 1929	Romani, piano	Unpublished radio broadcast
Baltimore 21 October 1954	Chicagov, piano	LP: Ed Smith ASCO 125 LP: Felmain FM 01 CD: Romophone 810 222

VINCENZO CIAMPI (1719-1762)

Tre giorni son che Nina

Baltimore 19 October 1954	Chicagov, piano	LP: Ed Smith ASCO 125 CD: Romophone 810 222 Published recording comprises 2 takes

FRANCESCO CILEA (1866-1950)

Adriana Lecouvreur, excerpt (Io son l'umile ancella)

Baltimore 7 April 1950	Private acetate
Baltimore 5 September 1953	LP: Ed Smith EJS 243/ANNA 1036 LP: Collectors Limited Edition MDP 036

Adriana Lecouvreur, excerpt (Poveri fiori)

Baltimore 7 April 1950	Private acetate
Baltimore 5 September 1953	LP: Ed Smith EJS 243/ANNA 1036 LP: Collectors Limited Edition MDP 036

HENRY CLOUGH-LEITER (1874-1956)

My lover he comes on a ski

New York 11 December 1933	Unpublished radio broadcast

GIOVANNI DE CURTIS (1860-1926)

Carmè

Camden NJ 11 April 1924	Orchestra Bourdon	Victor 1013 CD: Nimbus NI 1777/NI 7805 CD: Romophone 810 062
New York 10 December 1936	Orchestra Kelsey	CD: Eklipse EKRCD 51

CLAUDE DEBUSSY (1862-1918)

Beau soir

Baltimore 22 November 1953		Unpublished private recording
Baltimore 17 October 1954	Chicagov, piano	LP: Victor LM 2047 CD: Romophone 810 222

La chevelure

Baltimore 17 October 1954	Chicagov, piano	LP: Victor LM 2047 CD: Romophone 810 222

LEO DELIBES (1836-1891)

Bonjour Suzon!

Baltimore 17 October 1954	Chicagov, piano	LP: Victor LM 2047 CD: Romophone 810 222

LUIGI DENZA (1846-1922)

Se

Baltimore 18 October 1954	Chicagov, piano	LP: Ed Smith ASCO 125 LP: Felmain FM 01 CD: Romophone 810 222

EDUARDO DI CAPUA (1865-1917)

Maria Mari!

New York 26 July 1920	Orchestra Romani	Columbia 49870/68064D/7035M LP: Scala (USA) 838 CD: Nimbus NI 1771/NI 7805 CD: Pearl GEMMCDS 9644 CD: Vocal Archives VA 1120 CD: Minerva MNA 7
Camden NJ 23 January 1924	Orchestra Bourdon	Victor unpublished
Camden NJ 11 April 1924	Orchestra Bourdon	Victor 1013 CD: Romophone 810 062

O sole mio

New York 9 September 1921	C.Ponselle Orchestra Romani	Columbia 49983/9007M LP: Scala (USA) 851 CD: Pearl GEMMCDS 9964 CD: Vocal Archives VA 1120 CD: Minerva MNA 7
New York 18 October 1931	Romani, piano	Unpublished radio broadcast

VINCENZO DI CHIARA (1860-1937)

La spagnola

Camden NJ 5 June 1925	Orchestra Pasternack Sung in English	Victor VA 69 LP: Ed Smith EJS 191 CD: Vocal Archives VA 1120 CD: Legato BIM 701 CD: Romophone 810 062 CD: Minerva MNA 7

STEFANO DONAUDY (1879-1925)

O del mio amato ben

Baltimore 19 October 1954	Chicagov, piano	LP: Victor LM 1889/L 16493 CD: Romophone 810 222

Freschi luoghi prati aulenti

New York 19 January 1933		Unpublished radio broadcast
New York 11 December 1933		Unpublished radio broadcast

HENRI DUPARC (1848-1933)

Extase

Baltimore 17 October 1954	Chicagov, piano	Victor unpublished

L'invitation au voyage

Baltimore 24 August 1953		Unpublished private recording
Baltimore 17 October 1954	Chicagov, piano	LP: Ed Smith EJS 243 CD: Romophone 810 222

GABRIEL DUPONT (1878-1914)

La rosita

Camden NJ 1 June 1925	Orchestra Pasternack Sung in English	Victor unpublished
Camden NJ 4 June 1925	Orchestra Pasternack Sung in English	Victor VA 69 LP: Ed Smith EJS 191 CD: Legato LCD 179 CD: Vocal Archives VA 1120 CD: Romophone 810 062 CD: Minerva MNA 7

1 June version was an acoustic recording, 4 June version was an electrical recording

ANTONIN DVORAK (1841-1904)

Songs my mother taught me

Camden NJ 17 January 1928	Orchestra Bourdon	Victor 1319 HMV DA 1023 LP: Pearl GEMM 207 CD: Romophone 810 072

Humoresque, arrangement

New York 18 March 1936	Orchestra and Chorus Kostelanetz	LP: Ed Smith EJS 192 CD: Vocal Archives VA 1120

Unpublished radio broadcast, dated 5 November 1934, may also survive

CARL ANTON ECKERT (1820-1879)

Swiss echo song

New York 3 December 1928	Romani, piano	Unpublished radio broadcast
New York 7 December 1930	Romani, piano	Unpublished radio broadcast

Unpublished radio broadcasts of the song dated 13 October 1929, 10 April 1930, 3 March 1933 and 22 January 1933 may also survive

ROGER EDENS (Born 1905)

What is in the air today?

New York 26 November 1934	Orchestra Kostelanetz	LP: Ed Smith EJS 243

MANUEL DE FALLA (1876-1946)

Asturiana/7 canciones populares espanolas

Baltimore 18 October 1954	Chicagov, piano	CD: Romophone 810 222

Nana/7 canciones populares espanolas

Baltimore 18 October 1954	Chicagov, piano	LP: Ed Smith ASCO 125 CD: Romophone 810 222

RODOLFO FALVO (1874-1936)

Dicitencello vuje

New York 27 September 1936	Orchestra Rapee	LP: Ed Smith EJS 191 LP: Collectors Limited Edition MDP 012
Baltimore 21 October 1954	Ponselle, piano	LP: Victor LM 2047 CD: Romophone 810 222

ROLAND FARLEY

The night wind

New York 13 October 1929	Romani, piano	Unpublished radio broadcast
New York 10 April 1930		Unpublished radio broadcast
New York 18 October 1931	Romani, piano	Unpublished radio broadcast
Washington 3 March 1933		Unpublished radio broadcast
New York 25 March 1936	Orchestra Kostelanetz	LP: Ed Smith EJS 192
Cincinatti 25 April 1937	Cincinatti SO Goossens	CD: Eklipse EKRCD 51
Baltimore 19 October 1954	Chicagov, piano	First version CD: Romophone 810 222 Second version LP: Victor LM 1889/L 16493 LP: OASI 635 CD: Romophone 810 222

Other radio broadcasts of this song may survive

GABRIEL FAURE (1845-1924)

Après un rêve

Baltimore 15 May 1950	Unnamed pianist	LP: Ed Smith EJS 191

Unpublished private recording dated 18 February 1953 may also survive

FRIEDRICH FLOTOW (1812-1883)

Martha, excerpt (Letzte Rose)

New York 29 October 1934	Orchestra Sung in English	Unpublished radio broadcast

NICHOLAS DE FONTENAILLES

A l'aimé

Hollywood 31 October 1939	Romani, piano	Victor 2053 LP: Victor CBL 100/CDN 1006-1007 CD: RCA/BMG GD 87810 CD: Romophone 810 222 CD: Nimbus NI 7839

STEPHEN FOSTER (1826-1864)

My old Kentucky home

Camden 2 June 1925	Male Voice Quartet Orchestra Pasternack	Victor 6509 CD: Nimbus NI 1771/NI 7878 CD: Romophone 810 062 Ponselle's first published electrical recording
New York 13 October 1929	Romani, piano	Unpublished radio broadcast

The old folks at home

New York 15 February 1921	Orchestra Romani	Columbia 49934/68065D/7064M CD: Pearl GEMMCDS 9964
Camden NJ 3 June 1925	Orchestra Pasternack	Victor unpublished
Camden NJ 4 June 1925	Orchestra Pasternack	First version International Record Collectors Club 126 LP: Pearl GEMM 207 CD: Nimbus NI 1771/NI 7878 CD: Romophone 810 062 Second version HMV DB 872 CD: Romophone 810 062
Baltimore 25 September 1950	J.C.Thomas and piano accompaniment	LP: Rosa Ponselle GR 101 LP: Ed Smith EJS 531 CD: Eklipse EKRCD 51 CD: Legato LCD 139 Eklipse and Legato dated 1950
Baltimore 3 April 1953		Unpublished private recording

CESAR FRANCK (1822-1890)

Panis angelicus

Baltimore 20 October 1954	Chicagov, piano	Victor unpublished

RUDOLF FRIML (1879-1972)

Rose Marie, excerpt (Indian love call)

New York 22 January 1933		Unpublished radio broadcast

CHRISTOPH WILLIBALD GLUCK (1714-1787)

Alceste, excerpt (Divinités du Styx!)

New York 3 December 1934	Orchestra Kostelanetz	LP: Ed Smith EJS 103-104/EJS 190/ ANNA 1036 LP: Collectors Limited Edition MDP 012

Unpublished radio broadcasts of the aria dated 19 January 1933, 9 June 1934 and 31 May 1936 may also survive

ENRIQUE GRANADOS (1867-1916)

El mirar de la maja

Baltimore 18 October 1954	Chicagov, piano	LP: Victor LM 2047 CD: Romophone 810 222

EDVARD GRIEG (1843-1907)

Ich liebe dich

New York 19 February 1933		Unpublished radio broadcast
New York 25 March 1936		Unpublished radio broadcast

GROSVENER

Here's to Romance, excerpt (I carry you in my pocket)

New York 26 February 1936	Orchestra Kostelanetz	LP: Ed Smith EJS 192 LP: Collectors Limited Edition MDP 012 CD: Vocal Archives VA 1120

Unpublished radio broadcasts dated 7 May 1934 and 25 June 1934 may also survive

FRANZ XAVER GRUBER (1787-1863)

Stille Nacht heilige Nacht

Baltimore 1953	C.Ponselle	LP: Legendary LR 139 Introduced by Rosa Ponselle

JACQUES HALEVY (1799-1862)

La juive, excerpt (Il va venir)

New York 28 March 1923	Orchestra Romani	Columbia unpublished
New York 11 January 1924	Orchestra Romani	Columbia AF 1 LP: Scala (USA) 838 CD: Nimbus NI 1771/NI 7846 CD: Pearl GEMMCDS 9964 CD: Musique memoria MM 31071
New York 14 January 1924	Orchestra Romani	Columbia unpublished

HAWTHORNE

Whispering hope

New York 1 March- 9 July 1919	B.Maurel Orchestra Romani	Columbia 78325/36000D/2019M Columbia (UK) X 242 LP: Scala (USA) 838

MICHAEL HEAD (1900-1976)

Slumber song of the Madonna

New York 11 December 1933		Unpublished radio broadcast

VICTOR HERBERT (1859-1924)

Mademoiselle Modiste, excerpt (Kiss me again)

New York 26 July 1920	Orchestra Romani	Columbia 49869/68077D/7061M LP: Scala (USA) 838 CD: Pearl GEMMCDS 9964 CD: Nimbus NI 1771/NI 7846/NI 7851 CD: Metropolitan Opera MET 218
New York 10 April 1930		Unpublished radio broadcast
New York 28 January 1934	Orchestra Shilkret	Unpublished radio broadcast
New York 10 December 1936	Orchestra Kelsey	CD: Eklipse EKRCD 51
New York 2 May 1937	Orchestra Black	LP: Ed Smith EJS 192 CD: Nimbus NI 1777/NI 7846/NI 7851 CD: Vocal Archives VA 1120

Naughty Marietta, excerpt (Ah sweet mystery of life!)

New York 22 January 1933		Unpublished radio broadcast
New York 28 January 1934	Orchestra Shilkret	Unpublished radio broadcast
New York 30 April 1934		Unpublished radio broadcast

JOHN HILL HEWITT (1801-1890)

The little old garden

Camden NJ 1 June 1925	Orchestra Pasternack	Victor VA 67 LP: Ed Smith EJS 192/EJS 397 CD: Legato LCD 179 CD: Vocal archives VA 1120 CD: Romophone 810 062 CD: Minerva MNA 7

LOUIS HIRSCH (1881-1924)

Carolina sunshine

New York 15 January 1920	Orchestra Romani	Columbia 78927 This recording was not published

CARRIE JACOBS BOND (1862-1946)

A perfect day

Camden NJ 3-4 June 1925	Orchestra Pasternack	Victor 1098 CD: Nimbus NI 1771/NI 7805 CD: Romophone 810 062

I love you truly

New York 1 October 1934	Orchestra Kostelanetz	LP: Ed Smith EJS 192 CD: Vocal Archives VA 1120

NICOLO JOMMELLI (1714-1774)

Chi vuol comprar

New York 19 January 1933		Unpublished radio broadcast

PERCY KAHN (1880-1966)

Ave Maria

Camden NJ 2-16 June 1927	Orchestra Bourdon	Victor 1456 LP: Victor CBL 100/CDN 1006-1007 CD: Romophone 810 072
Cincinatti 25 April 1937	Cincinatti SO Goossens	LP: OASI 635 CD: Eklipse EKRCD 51

FRANCIS SCOTT KEY (1779-1843)

The star-spangled banner, arrangement

Baltimore 25 September 1952		LP: Collectors Limited Edition MDP 036 CD: Eklipse EKRCD 51
Baltimore 4 October 1952		Unpublished private recording

ERICH WOLFGANG KORNGOLD (1897-1957)

Die tote Stadt, excerpt (Glück das mir verblieb)

New York 19 January 1933	Harlem PO	Unpublished radio broadcast
Washington 3 March 1933	National SO Kindler	Unpublished radio broadcast
New York 11 December 1933		Unpublished radio broadcast
New York 30 April 1934		Unpublished radio broadcast
Baltimore 27 October 1954	Ponselle, piano	LP: Ponselle by Request RPX 102 LP: Ed Smith EJS 243/ANNA 1037 LP: Collectors Limited Edition MDP 036

LAFORGE

Come unto these yellow sands

New York 23 October 1930		Unpublished radio broadcast
New York 19 January 1933		Unpublished radio broadcast
New York 23 April 1934		Unpublished radio broadcast

CHARLES LECOCQ (1832-1913)

La chanson de la cigale

New York 13 October 1929	Romani, piano	Unpublished radio broadcast

FRANZ LEHAR (1870-1948)

The Merry Widow waltz

New York 12 March 1933		Unpublished radio broadcast
New York 19 November 1934		Unpublished radio broadcast

LIZA LEHMANN (1862-1918)

The cuckoo

New York 7 December 1930	Romani, piano	Unpublished radio broadcast
New York 1 April 1936	Orchestra Kostelanetz	LP: Ed Smith EJS 192 CD: Vocal Archives VA 1120

RUGGERO LEONCAVALLO (1858-1919)

I pagliacci, excerpt (Stridono lassù)

New York 13 February 1922	Orchestra Romani	Columbia unpublished
New York 22 September 1923	Orchestra Romani	Columbia unpublished
New York 11 January 1924	Orchestra Romani	Columbia 98063/68084D/7066M LP: Scala (USA) 851 CD: Pearl GEMMCDS 9964 CD: Nimbus NI 1771/NI 7878 CD: Metropolitan Opera MET 218

THURLOE LIEURANCE (1878-1963)

By the waters of Minnetonka

New York 10 April 1930		Unpublished radio broadcast

FRANZ LISZT (1811-1886)

O lieb solang du lieben kannst

New York 19 March 1933		Unpublished radio broadcast

LOCKHART MANNING

In the Luxembourg gardens

Baltimore 19 October 1954	Chicagov, piano	LP: Ed Smith EJS 247 CD: Romophone 810 222

Unpublished radio broadcasts of the song dated 23 October 1930, 12 March 1933 and 19 March 1933 may also survive

HERMANN LOEHR (1871-1943)

Rose of my heart

New York 17 September 1921	Orchestra Romani	Columbia 49987 This recording was not published
New York 13 April 1922	Orchestra Romani	Columbia 80307/33003D/2024M LP: Scala (USA) 851 CD: Pearl GEMMCDS 9964

Where my caravan has rested

New York 2-13 June 1922	C.Ponselle Orchestra Romani	Columbia 80392/36002D/2019M LP: Scala (USA) 851 CD: Pearl GEMMCDS 9964

JEAN-BAPTISTE LULLY (1632-1687)

Amadis, excerpt (Bois épais)

Baltimore 4 October 1952		Unpublished radio vroadcast
Baltimore 16 October 1954	Chicagov, piano	LP: Victor LM 1889/L 16493 CD: Romophone 810 222

LUZZI

Ave Maria

Baltimore 7 December 1953	Chicagov, piano	LP: Ed Smith EJS 191
Baltimore 20 October 1954	Chicagov, piano	CD: Romophone 810 222

MANNA-ZUCCA

Rachem

New York 8 January 1921	Orchestra Romani Sung in Yiddish	Columbia 49925/7025M LP: Scala (USA) 851 CD: Pearl GEMMCDS 9964

JOHANN MARTINI (1741-1816)

Baltimore 28 June 1954		Unpublished private recording
Baltimore 17 October 1954	Chicagov, piano	LP: Victor LM 2047 CD: Romophone 810 222

PIETRO MASCAGNI (1863-1945)

L'amico Fritz, excerpt (Son pochi fiori)

Baltimore 24 August 1953		Unpublished private recording

Cavalleria rusticana, excerpt (Voi lo sapete)

New York 9 January 1919	Orchestra Romani	Columbia 49570/68039D/8909M LP: Ember GVC 9 LP: Scala (USA) 838 CD: Nimbus NI 1771/NI 7846 CD: Pearl GEMMCDS 9964 CD: Metropolitan Opera MET 218 GVC 9 incorrectly dated December 1919
New York 28 January 1934	Orchestra Shilkret	Unpublished radio broadcast
New York 11 March 1936	Orchestra Kostelanetz	LP: Ed Smith EJS 170/EJS 190/UORC 118/ ANNA 1036/ASCO 125 LP: Collectors Limited Edition MDP 012

Cavalleria rusticana, Intermezzo arrangement

New York 29 November 1918	Orchestra Romani	Columbia 49556 This recording was not published
New York 8 October 1934	Orchestra Kostelanetz	LP: Ed Smith EJS 532 LP: Collectors Limited Edition MDP 029

JULES MASSENET (1842-1912)

Manon, excerpt (Adieu notre petite table)

Baltimore 24 November 1952	Ponselle, piano	LP: Ed Smith EJS 243/ANNA 1037 LP: Collectors Limited Edition MDP 036

Elégie

Camden NJ 19 May 1926	Lennartz, cello Orchestra Bourdon	First version Victor 6599 HMV DB 1052 45: Victor WCT 12 LP: Victor LCT 1008/CBL 100/ CDN 1006-1007 CD: Nimbus NI 1771/NI 7846 CD: Romophone 810 072 Second version Victor 6599 CD: Romophone 810 072
New York 1 January 1927	Orchestra Shilkret	Unpublished radio broadcast Probably Ponselle's radio debut
New York 7 December 1930	Orchestra Pasternack	Unpublished radio broadcast
New York 27 March 1932		Unpublished radio broadcast
Baltimore 18 May 1953		Unpublished private recording

ANDRE MESSAGER (1853-1929)

Fortunio, excerpt (J'aimais la vieille maison grise)

Baltimore 30 March 1957	Chicagov, piano	LP: Ponselle by Request RPX 102 LP: Ed Smith EJS 243 LP: Collectors Limited Edition MDP 036 MDP 036 dated 1953

GIACOMO MEYERBEER (1791-1864)

L'africaine

New York 13 January 1934	Role of Selika Morgana, Jagel, A.Borgioli Metropolitan Opera Orchestra & Chorus Serafin Sung in Italian	Unpublished Met broadcast

L'africaine, excerpt (Fils du soleil!)

New York 1 February 1923	Orchestra Romani Sung in Italian	Columbia 98059/68000D LP: Scala (USA) 851 CD: Pearl GEMMCDS 9964
Camden NJ 14 January 1925	Orchestra Bourdon Sung in Italian	First version Victor 6496 CD: Metropolitan Opera MET 218 CD: Romophone 810 062 Second version LP: Victor CBL 100/CDN 1006-1007 LP: Preiser LV 297 CD: Nimbus NI 1771/NI 7878 CD: RCA/BMG GD 87810 CD: Romophone 810 062

HARRISON MILLARD (1830-1895)

Ave Maria

Baltimore 20 October 1954	Chicagov, piano	CD: Romophone 810 222

METROPOLITAN OPERA HOUSE

GRAND OPERA SEASON 1929-1930
GIULIO GATTI-CASAZZA, GENERAL MANAGER

MONDAY EVENING, JANUARY 6, AT 8 O'CLOCK

DON GIOVANNI

OPERA IN TWO ACTS (TEN SCENES)
(IN ITALIAN)
BOOK BY LORENZO DA PONTE

MUSIC BY WOLFGANG AMADEUS MOZART

DON GIOVANNI	EZIO PINZA
DONNA ANNA	ROSA PONSELLE
IL COMMENDATORE	LEON ROTHIER
DON OTTAVIO	BENIAMINO GIGLI
DONNA ELVIRA	ELISABETH RETHBERG
ZERLINA	EDITHA FLEISCHER
LEPORELLO	PAVEL LUDIKAR
MASETTO	LOUIS D'ANGELO

Minuet by CORPS DE BALLET
Arranged by AUGUST BERGER

CONDUCTOR.......TULLIO SERAFIN

STAGE DIRECTOR.......WILHELM VON WYMETAL
CHORUS MASTER.......GIULIO SETTI
STAGE MANAGER.......ARMANDO AGNINI

NEW SCENIC PRODUCTION BY JOSEPH URBAN

Positively No Encores Allowed

Program Continued on Next Page

"His Master's Voice"
NEW RECORDS
ROSA PONSELLE (Soprano).
Photo: C. Mishkin, N.Y (See Page 2).
FIRST JUNE 1929
"His Master's Voice"
ELECTRICAL RECORDING

WILLIAM HENRY MONK (1823-1889)

Abide with me

New York 9 July 1919	B.Maurel Orchestra Romani	Columbia 78557/36000D Columbia (UK) X 245 LP: Scala (USA) 851

GEORGE MONRO (Died 1731)

My lovely Celia

Camden NJ 11 April 1924	Orchestra Bourdon	Victor 1057 CD: Romophone 810 062
Baltimore 18 October 1954	Chicagov, piano	LP: Ed Smith ASCO 125 CD: Romophone 810 222

THOMAS MOORE (1779-1852)

The last rose of summer

New York 27 March 1932		Unpublished radio broadcast

MORITZ MOSZKOWSKI (1854-1925)

Serenade, arrangement

New York 19 March 1933		Unpublished radio broadcast

WOLFGANG AMADEUS MOZART (1756-1791)

Don Giovanni

New York 17 December 1932	Role of Anna Müller, Fleischer, Schipa, Pinza, Pasero, Malatesta, Rothier Metropolitan Opera Orchestra & Chorus Serafin	Unpublished Met broadcast
New York 20 January 1934	Müller, Fleischer, Schipa, Pinza, Lazzari, D'Angelo List Metropolitan Opera Orchestra & Chorus Serafin	Unpublished Met broadcast Excerpts LP: Ed Smith ANNA 1036
New York 9 February 1935	Müller, Fleischer, Schipa, Pinza, Lazzari, D'Angelo, List Metropolitan Opera Orchestra & Chorus Panizza	Unpublished Met broadcast

Don Giovanni, excerpt (Batti batti)

New York 1 October 1934	Orchestra Kostelanetz	LP: Ed Smith EJS 103-104/EJS 190/ ANNA 1036 LP: Collectors Limited Edition MDP 012

Don Giovanni, excerpt (Là ci darem la mano)

Baltimore 8 May 1953	Pinza Piano acc.	LP: Ed Smith EJS 243/ANNA 1037 LP: Collectors Limited Edition MDP 012
Baltimore 22 April 1954	Hecht Piano acc.	Unpublished private recording

Le nozze di Figaro, excerpt (Voi che sapete)

Baltimore 21 October 1954		LP: Ed Smith ASCO 125 CD: Romophone 810 222

MODEST MUSSORGSKY (1839-1881)

With the doll/The nursery

New York 19 January 1933		Unpublished radio broadcast

ETHELBERT NEVIN (1862-1901)

Mighty like a rose

New York 3 December 1928	Romani, piano	Unpublished radio broadcast
New York 22 January 1933		Unpublished radio broadcast

Oh that we two were maying

New York 9 June 1922	C.Ponselle Romani, piano	Columbia 80391 This recording was not published

The rosary

Camden NJ 3-4 June 1925	Orchestra Pasternack	Victor unpublished
Camden NJ 5 June 1925	Orchestra Pasternack	Victor 1098 CD: Romophone 810 062
New York 1 January 1927	Orchestra Shilkret	Unpublished radio broadcast Probably Ponselle's radio debut

Further unpublished radio broadcasts of the song dated 10 April 1930 and 27 March 1932 may also survive

IVOR NOVELLO (1893-1951)

Keep the home fires burning

New York 15 February 1919	Harrison, Miller, Croxton, Sarto Orchestra Romani	Columbia 49585/7038M LP: Scala (USA) 851 LP: Oasi OASI 619 CD: Pearl GEMMCDS 9964 CD: Vocal Archives VA 1120 CD: Minerva MNA 7

JACQUES OFFENBACH (1819-1880)

Les contes d'Hoffmann, excerpt (Belle nuit, o nuit d'amour)

New York 9 December 1919	C.Ponselle Orchestra Romani Sung in English	Columbia 78846/36001D LP: Scala (USA) 838 CD: Pearl GEMMCDS 9964
Baltimore 22 July 1951	C.Ponselle	Unpublished private recording

GIOVANNI PAISIELLO (1740-1816)

La molinara, excerpt (Nel cor più non mi sento)

Baltimore 18 October 1954	Chicagov, piano	LP: Victor LM 2047 CD: Romophone 810 222

Unpublished private recordings of the aria dated January 1951 and 6 March 1953 may also survive

EMIL PALADILHE (1844-1926)

Psyché

Baltimore 28 June 1954		Unpublished private recording
Baltimore 21 October 1954	Chicagov, piano	LP: Ed Smith ASCO 125

MARIO PERSICO

Rosemonde

Baltimore 17 October 1954	Chicagov, piano	LP: Victor LM 1889/L 16493 CD: Romophone 810 222

AMILCARE PONCHIELLI (1834-1886)

La Gioconda, excerpt (Suicidio!)

New York 14 January 1920	Orchestra Romani	Columbia 49735/68039D/7034M LP: Scala (USA) 803 LP: Ember GVC 9 LP: Rhapsody RHA 6007 CD: Metropolitan Opera MET 218
New York 11 October 1923	Orchestra Romani	CD: Pearl GEMMCDS 9964
Camden NJ 14 January 1925	Orchestra Bourdon	First version Victor 6496 HMV DB 854 LP: Victor TVM 17202/CBL 100/ CDN 1006-1007 LP: Preiser LV 297 CD: RCA/BMG GD 87810 CD: Nimbus NI 1777/NI 7805 CD: Romophone 810 062 Second version CD: Romophone 810 062

GIACOMO PUCCINI (1858-1924)

La Bohème, excerpt (Si mi chiamano Mimì)

New York 13 February 1923	Orchestra Romani	Columbia 98062/68000D/7035M LP: Scala (USA) 803 LP: Ember GVC 9 CD: Nimbus NI 1777/NI 7878 CD: Pearl GEMMCDS 9964 GVC 9 incorrectly dated January 1924

La Bohème, excerpt (Sono andati)

Baltimore 23 October 1954		Unpublished private recording Recording incomplete

Madama Butterfly, excerpt (Un bel dì)

New York 9 January 1919	Orchestra Romani	Columbia 49571/68059D/7065M/5095M Columbia (UK) 7234/7340 LP: Scala (USA) 803 LP: Ember GVC 9 CD: Nimbus NI 1777/NI 7802/NI 7846 CD: Pearl GEMMCDS 9964 GVC 9 incorrectly dated May 1919

Manon Lescaut, excerpt (In quelle trine morbide)

New York 7 September 1921	Orchestra Romani	Columbia 79971/36001D/2014M/CRS 15 LP: Scala (USA) 803 LP: Ember GVC 9 CD: Metropolitan Opera MET 218 CD: Pearl GEMMCDS 9964 GVC 9 incorrectly dated January 1923
New York 19 September- 11 October 1923	Orchestra Romani	Columbia 79971/36001D/2014M LP: Scala (USA) 851 CD: Nimbus NI 1777/NI 7846 CD: Pearl GEMMCDS 9964 This recording includes preceding recitative

Suor Angelica, excerpt (Senza mamma)

Baltimore 13 September 1952		Unpublished private recording
Baltimore 1954		LP: Ed Smith ANNA 1037

Tosca, excerpt (Vissi d'arte)

New York 7 January 1919	Orchestra Romani	Columbia 49569/68059D/7065M/5095M LP: Scala (USA) 803 LP: Ember GVC 9 CD: Nimbus NI 1777/NI 7846/NI 7851 CD: Pearl GEMMCDS 9964 GVC 9 incorrectly dated December 1921

MAX REGER (1873-1916)

Mariae Wiegenlied

New York 7 December 1930	Romani, piano	Unpublished radio broadcast

Unpublished radio broadcasts of the song dated 27 March 1932 and 24 December 1933 may also survive

TERESA DEL RIEGO (1876-1968)

Homing

New York 1 October 1934		Unpublished radio broadcast
New York 27 September 1936	Orchestra Rapee	LP: Ed Smith EJS 191
Baltimore 19 October 1954	Chicagov, piano	LP: Victor LM 1889/L 16493 CD: Romophone 810 222

NIKOLAI RIMSKY-KORSAKOV (1844-1908)

The nightingale and the rose

Camden NJ 2 June 1927	Barone, flute Orchestra Bourdon Sung in English	Victor 1456 LP: Victor CBL 100/CDN 1006-1007 CD: Romophone 810 072
New York 22 January 1933		Unpublished radio broadcast
Hollywood 31 October 1939	Romani, piano Sung in English	Victor 16451 LP: Felmain FM 09 CD: RCA/BMG GD 87810 CD: Vocal Archives VA 1120 CD: Nimbus NI 1777/NI 7805 CD: Romophon 810 222 CD: Minerva MNA 7

Sadko, excerpt (Song of the Indian guest)

New York 30 December 1920	Orchestra Romani Sung in English	Columbia 49920/68077D/7061M LP: Scala (USA) 838 CD: Nimbus NI 1777/NI 7846 CD: Pearl GEMMCDS 9964

RICHARD RODGERS (1902-1979)

So in love

Baltimore 23 May 1952		Unpublished private recording

Some enchanted evening

Baltimore 25 September 1952		CD: Eklipse EKRCD 51
Baltimore 3 May 1953		Unpublished private recording

ROMANO ROMANI

Fedra, excerpt (O divina Afrodite!)

New York 7 December 1930	Orchestra Romani	Unpublished radio broadcast
New York 18 October 1931	Orchestra Pasternack	Unpublished radio broadcast
New York 18 March 1936	Orchestra Kostelanetz	LP: Ed Smith EJS 103-104 LP: Collectors Limited Edition MDP 012
New York 2 May 1937	Orchestra Black	LP: Ed Smith EJS 141/EJS 190/ANNA 1036

Unpublished radio broadcasts of the aria dated 2 April 1934 and 10 December 1934 may also survive

GIOACHINO ROSSINI (1792-1868)

Guillaume Tell, excerpt (Sombres forêts)

New York 1 February 1923	Orchestra Romani Sung in Italian	Columbia 98058/68058D/7026M/CRS 15 LP: Scala (USA) 803 LP: Ember GVC 9 CD: Nimbus NI 1777/NI 7846 CD: Pearl GEMMCDS 9964 CD: Metropolitan Opera MET 218 GVC 9 incorrectly dated November 1923

Semiramide, excerpt (Bel raggio lusinghier)

Los Angeles 24 May 1936	Los Angeles PO Rapee	LP: Ed Smith EJS 103-104/EJS 190/ ANNA 1036 LP: Collectors Limited Edition MDP 012

ANTON RUBINSTEIN (1829-1894)

Since I first met thee

Camden NJ 17 January 1928	Lennartz, cello Orchestra Bourdon	Victor 1319 HMV DA 1023 LP: Pearl GEMM 207 CD: Romophone 810 072

GENI SADERO (1886-1961)

Amuri amuri

Baltimore 17 October 1954	Ponselle, piano	LP: Victor LM 1889/L 16493 CD: RCA/BMG GD 87810 CD: Romophone 810 222

Unpublished private recordings of the song dated 10 January 1951, 27 June 1951 and 28 June 1954 may also survive

Battitori di grano

Baltimore 17 October 1954	Chicagov, piano	First version LP: Victor LM 1889/L 16493 CD: Romophone 810 222 Second version CD: Romophone 810 222

Fa la nana bambin

New York 3 December 1928	Romani, piano	Unpublished radio broadcast
Baltimore 27 June 1951		Unpublished private recording
Baltimore 27 October 1951		Unpublished private recording
Baltimore 1 June 1952		Unpublished radio broadcast 2 takes recorded; sung in English
Baltimore 28 June 1954		Unpublished private recording
Baltimore 17 October 1954	Ponselle, piano	LP: Victor LM 2047 CD: Romophone 810 222

CAMILLE SAINT-SAENS (1835-1921)

Samson et Dalila, excerpt (Amour viens aider ma faiblesse!)

Baltimore 19 October 1953		Unpublished private recording
Baltimore 7 November 1953	Lawrence, piano	LP: Ed Smith EJS 243/ANNA 1037 LP: Ponselle by Request RPX 102 LP: Collectors Limited Edition MDP 036

Samson et Dalila, excerpt (Mon coeur s'ouvre à ta voix)

Baltimore 19 October 1953		Unpublished private recording
Baltimore 7 November 1953	Lawrence, piano	LP: Ed Smith EJS 243 LP: Ponselle by Request RPX 102 LP: Collectors Limited Edition MDP 036

Samson et Dalila, excerpt (Printemps qui commence)

New York 29 October 1934	Orchestra Kostelanetz	LP: Ed Smith EJS 243/ANNA 1037 LP: Collectors Limited Edition MDP 012 ANNA 1037 incorrectly dated November 1953
Baltimore 7 November 1953	Lawrence, piano	LP: Collectors Limited Edition MDP 036

Guitares et mandolines

Baltimore 20 October 1954	Chicagov, piano	LP: Victor LM 1889/L 16493 CD: Romophone 810 222

MIGUEL SANDOVAL (1903-1953)

Ave Maria

New York 25 March 1936	Orchestra Kostelanetz	LP: Ed Smith EJS 103-104/EJS 191
Baltimore 20 October 1954	Chicagov, piano	CD: Romophone 810 222

FRANZ SCHUBERT (1797-1828)

An die Musik

Baltimore 5 September 1953		Unpublished private recording
Baltimore 20 October 1954	Chicagov, piano	LP: Ed Smith EJS 243 CD: Romophone 810 222

Ave Maria

New York 27 March 1932		Unpublished radio broadcast
Hollywood 1 November 1939	M.Schmidt, violin Romani, piano Sung in Latin	Victor VB 74 CD: Nimbus NI 7861 CD: Metropolitan Opera MET 206 CD: Romophone 810 222
Hollywood 7 November 1939	M.Schmidt, violin Romani, piano Sung in Latin	CD: Romophone 810 222
Washington 28 October 1950		Unpublished private recording
Baltimore December 1950		Unpublished private recording
Baltimore 16 January 1951		Unpublished private recording
Baltimore 25 September 1952		CD: Eklipse EKRCD 51

Erlkönig

New York 4 March 1936	Orchestra Kostelanetz	LP: Ed Smith EJS 191 LP: Collectors Limited Edition MDP 012
Baltimore 5 September 1953		Unpublished private recording
Baltimore 19 October 1954	Chicagov, piano	LP: Victor LM 1889/L 16493 CD: Romophone 810 222

Unpublished radio broadcasts of the song dated 3 March 1933, 24 December 1933, 11 June 1934 and 17 December 1934 may also survive

Nacht und Träume

Baltimore 24 August 1953		Unpublished private recording

Ständchen

Camden NJ 19 May 1926	C.Ponselle Orchestra Bourdon	LP: Victor VIC 1507 LP: Ed Smith ANNA 1072 CD: Romophone 810 072 Composite transfer from 2 partially defective takes
New York 7 December 1930	Orchestra Pasternack	LP: Ed Smith EJS 452 Recording incomplete
New York 18 October 1931	Orchestra Pasternack	Unpublished radio broadcast
New York 22 January 1933		Unpublished radio broadcast
Baltimore 15 April 1950	Romani, piano	Unpublished private recording

A version of the song dated 1936-1937 was published on the LP OASI 635

Der Tod und das Mädchen

Baltimore 22 November 1953		Unpublished private recording
Baltimore 18 October 1954	Chicagov, piano	LP: Ed Smith ASCO 125 CD: Romophone 810 222

ROBERT SCHUMANN (1810-1856)

Der Nussbaum

Baltimore 22 October 1953		Unpublished private recording

Widmung

New York 19 January 1933		Unpublished radio broadcast

CYRIL SCOTT (1879-1970)

Annie Laurie

New York 7 December 1930	Romani, piano	Unpublished radio broadcast
New York 31 May 1936		LP: OASI 635 CD: Vocal Archives VA 1120

Unpublished radio broadcasts dated 12 March 1933 and 25 June 1934 may also survive

Lullaby

Camden NJ 23 January 1924	Orchestra Bourdon	Victor unpublished
Camden NJ 8 February 1924	Orchestra Bourdon	Victor 1002/66241 CD: Metropolitan Opera MET 218 CD: Romophone 810 062

Unpublished radio broadcast dated 12 March 1933 may also survive

HARRY ROWE SHELLEY (1858-1947)

Love's sorrow

Camden NJ 11 April 1924	Orchestra Bourdon	Victor 1057 CD: Romophone 810 062

RHEA SILBERTA (1900-1959)

Beloved

Camden NJ 1-4 June 1925	Orchestra Pasternack	Victor unpublished
Camden NJ 5 June 1925	Orchestra Pasternack	Victor VA 67 LP: Ed Smith EJS 192 CD: Romophone 810 062

1-4 June version was an acoustical recording, 5 June version was an electrical recording

GASPARE SPONTINI (1774-1851)

La vestale

Florence 7 May 1933	Role of Giulia Stignani, Dolci, Pasero, Pierobrasini Maggio musicale Orchestra & Chorus Gui	Unpublished radio broadcast

La vestale, excerpt (Tu che invoco)

Camden NJ 18 May 1926	Orchestra Bourdon	Victor 6605/VB 3 HMV DB 1274 LP: Victor TVM 17202/CBL 100/ CDN 1006-1007 LP: Pearl GEMM 207 CD: Nimbus NI 1777/NI 7805 CD: Metropolitan Opera MET 218 CD: Romophone 810 072
New York 19 March 1933		Unpublished radio broadcast
New York 1 April 1936	Orchestra Kostelanetz	LP: Ed Smith EJS 190 LP: Collectors Limited Edition MDP 012

La vestale, excerpt (O nume tutelar)

Camden NJ 18 May 1926	Orchestra Bourdon	First version Victor 6605/VB 3 HMV DB 1274 LP: Victor TVM 17202/CBL 100/ CDN 1006-1007 LP: Pearl GEMM 207 CD: RCA/BMG GD 87810 CD: Nimbus NI 1777/NI 7805 CD: Romophone 810 072 Second version CD: Romophone 810 072
New York 13 October 1929	Orchestra Pasternack	Unpublished radio broadcast
New York 11 December 1933		Unpublished radio broadcast

STARR

Little Alabama coon

New York 10 September 1921	Harrison, Miller, Croxton Orchestra Romani	Columbia unpublished
New York 13 April 1922	Harrison, Miller, Croxton Orchestra Romani	Columbia 79980/33003D/2024M LP: Scala (USA) 851 CD: Pearl GEMMCDS 9964

OSCAR STRAUS (1870-1954)

Der tapfere Soldat, excerpt (Komm Held meiner Träume!)

New York 19 February 1933		Unpublished radio broadcast
New York 8 October 1934	Orchestra Kostelanetz <u>Sung in English</u>	LP: Ed Smith EJS 532
Cincinatti 25 April 1937	Forest Cincinatti SO Goossens <u>Sung in English</u>	LP: OASI 635 CD: Vocal Archives VA 1120 CD: Eklipse EKRCD 51

JOHANN STRAUSS I (1825-1899)

An der schönen blauen Donau, arrangement

New York 17 September 1921	Orchestra Romani Sung in English	Columbia 49988/68078D/7062M LP: Scala (USA) 838 CD: Vocal Archives VA 1120 CD: Pearl GEMMCDS 9964 CD: Minerva MNA 7

G'schichten aus dem Wienerwald, arrangement

New York 5 November 1934		Unpublished radio broadcast

RICHARD STRAUSS (1864-1949)

Morgen

Baltimore 5 September 1953		Unpublished private recording
Baltimore 19 October 1954	Chicagov, piano	LP: Ed Smith ASCO 125 CD: Romophone 810 222

Wiegenlied

Baltimore 27 October 1951		Unpublished private recording

Zueignung

Baltimore January 1951		Unpublished private recording

STRELITZKI

Happy days

Camden NJ 1-5 June 1925	Victor unpublished

ARTHUR SULLIVAN (1842-1900)

My dearest heart

Camden NJ 1-5 June 1925	Victor unpublished

PIOTR TCHAIKOVSKY (1840-2893)

None but the lonely heart

New York 26 February 1936	Orchestra Kostelanetz Sung in German	LP: Ed Smith EJS 191
Cincinatti 25 April 1937	Cincinatti SO Goossens Sung in German	LP: OASI 635 CD: Eklipse EKRCD 51
Baltimore 15 April 1950	Romani, piano Sung in German	Unpublished private recording
Baltimore 28 June 1954		Unpublished private recording
Baltimore 16 October 1954	Chicagov, piano Sung in German	LP: Ed Smith ASCO 125 CD: Romophone 810 222

The Maid of Orleans, excerpt (Adieu forêts!)

New York 12 November 1934		Unpublished radio broadcast
New York 21 November 1935		Unpublished radio broadcast

PAOLO TOSTI (1846-1916)

'A vucchella

Camden NJ 18 May 1926	Orchestra Bourdon	Victor 1164 HMV DA 1035 LP: Victor CBL 100/CDN 1006-1007 CD: Nimbus NI 1777/NI 7878 CD: Metropolitan Opera MET 210 CD: Romophone 810 072 CD: Record Collector TRC 5
Baltimore 18 October 1954	Chicagov, piano	LP: Victor LM 2047 CD: Romophone 810 222

Aprile

Baltimore 18 October 1954	Chicagov, piano	LP: Victor LM 1889/L 16493 CD: Romophone 810 222

Ave Maria

Baltimore 20 October 1954	Chicagov, piano	LP: Ed Smith EJS 243 CD: Romophone 810 222

Addio

New York 2 December 1918	Orchestra Romani <u>Sung in English</u>	Columbia 49560/68064D/7038M LP: Scala (USA) 838 CD: Nimbus NI 1777/NI 7846 CD: Vocal Archives VA 1120 CD: Pearl GEMMCDS 9964 CD: Minerva MNA 7
Camden NJ 11 April 1924	Orchestra Bourdon <u>Sung in English</u>	<u>First version</u> CD: Romophone 810 062 <u>Second version</u> Victor 6453 LP: Victor CBL 100/CDN 1006-1007 CD: Romophone 810 062
Camden NJ 2 June 1927	Orchestra Bourdon <u>Sung in English</u>	Victor unpublished
Camden NJ 13 June 1927	Orchestra Bourdon <u>Sung in English</u>	Victor 6711 CD: Romophone 810 072
New York 19 February 1933		Unpublished radio broadcast
New York 24 December 1933		Unpublished radio broadcast
New York 1 April 1936	Orchestra Kostelanetz <u>Sung in English</u>	LP: Ed Smith EJS 191

Ideale

Baltimore 18 October 1954	Chicagov, piano	LP: Victor LM 2047 CD: Romophone 810 222

Luna d'estate

Camden NJ 18 May 1926	Orchestra Bourdon	Victor 1164/VA 68 HMV DA 1035 LP: Victor CBL 100/CDN 1006-1007 CD: Nimbus NI 1777/NI 7878 CD: Metropolitan Opera MET 218 CD: Romophone 810 072 CD: Musique memoria MM 31071

Marechiare

New York 18 October 1931	Romani, piano	Unpublished radio broadcast
New York 27 March 1932		Unpublished radio broadcast
Los Angeles 24 May 1936	Los Angeles PO Rapee	LP: Ed Smith EJS 191
Baltimore 18 October 1954	Ponselle, piano	LP: Victor LM 2047 CD: Romophone 810 222

La serenata

Camden NJ 12 April 1924	Lapitino, harp	First version Victor 6453 LP: Victor CBL 100/CDN 1006-1007 CD: Romophone 810 062 Second version CD: Nimbus NI 1777/NI 7878 CD: Romophone 810 062
Camden NJ 2 June 1927	Lapitino, harp	Victor 6711 CD: Romophone 810 072

Si tu le voulais

Hollywood 31 October 1939	Romani, piano	Victor 2053 LP: Victor CBL 100/CDN 1006-1007 CD: Nimbus NI 1777/NI 7878 CD: Romophone 810 222

Unpublished private recordings of the song dated 6 March 1953, 18 March 1953 and 18 February 1953 may also survive

L'ultima canzone

New York 11 March 1936	Orchestra Kostelanetz	LP: Ed Smith EJS 170/EJS 191/UORC 118 LP: Collectors Limited Edition MDP 012

Vorrei

Baltimore 1 October 1949		LP: Ed Smith EJS 532
Baltimore 14 December 1952		Unpublished private recording
Baltimore 21 October 1954	Chicagov, piano	LP: Victor LM 2047 CD: Romophone 810 222

RICHARD TRUNK (1879-1968)

Mir träumte von einem Königskind

Baltimore 15 April 1950	Romani, piano	Unpublished private recording
Baltimore January 1951		Unpublished private recording
Baltimore 18 October 1954	Chicagov, piano	LP: Victor LM 1889/L 16493 CD: Romophone 810 222

JOAQUIN VALVERDE (1846-1910)

Clavelitos

New York 12 November 1934		Unpublished radio broadcast
New York 4 March 1936	Orchestra Kostelanetz	LP: Ed Smith EJS 191

FREDERICK VANDERPOOL (1877-1947)

Values

New York 10 January 1920	Orchestra Romani	Columbia 78920 LP: Scala (USA) 838 CD: Pearl GEMMCDS 9964

FRANCESCO VERACINI (1690-1768)

Rosalinda, excerpt (Meco verrai)

New York 13 October 1929	Romani, piano	Unpublished radio broadcast

Madre pietosa vergine

New York 13 October 1929	Orchestra Pasternack	Unpublished radio broadcast

GIUSEPPE VERDI (1813-1901)

Aida, excerpt (Ritorna vincitor!)

New York 19 September 1923	Orchestra Romani	Columbia 98092/68084D/7066M LP: Scala (USA) 851 LP: Columbia Y 31150 LP: Preiser LV 297 CD: Nimbus NI 1777/NI 7878 CD: Pearl GEMMCDS 9964
Camden NJ 5 December 1923	Orchestra Bourdon	Victor 6437 LP: Victor VIC 1395 CD: Romophone 810 062
Camden NJ 11 December 1923	Orchestra Bourdon	CD: Romophone 810 062
Camden NJ 20 May 1926	Orchestra Bourdon	LP: Victor VIC 1507 CD: Romophone 810 072
Camden NJ 8 December 1927	Orchestra Bourdon	Victor unpublished
New York 1 January 1928	Metropolitan Opera Orchestra Setti	Unpublished radio broadcast
Camden NJ 18 January 1928	Orchestra Bourdon	Victor 7438/8993 HMV DB 1606 LP: Victor TVM 17202/PVM1-9047/ AG 26.41371 LP: Pearl GEMM 207 CD: Nimbus NI 1777/NI 7846 CD: RCA/BMG GD 87810 CD: Memoir CDMOIR 428 CD: Romophone 810 072
New York 19 February 1933		Unpublished radio broadcast
New York 27 September 1936	Orchestra Rapee	LP: Ed Smith EJS 169/EJS 190/ANNA 1036 LP: Collectors Limited Edition MDP 012 CD: Legato LCD 139

Aida, excerpt (O patria mia)

New York 29 November 1918	Orchestra Romani	Columbia 49557/68036D/8910M LP: Scala (USA) 838 LP: Columbia Y 31150 CD: Pearl GEMMCDS 9964 Y 31150 incorrectly dated 13 June 1922
Camden NJ 5 December 1923	Orchestra Bourdon	Victor 6437 HMV DB 854 LP: Top Artists' Platter TAP 306 LP: Pearl GEMM 207 LP: Preiser LV 297 CD: RCA/BMG GD 87810 CD: Nimbus NI 1777/NI 7805 CD: Metropolitan Opera MET 218 CD: Memoir CDMOIR 428 CD: Romophone 810 062
Camden NJ 11 December 1923	Orchestra Bourdon	Victor unpublished
Camden NJ 20 May 1926	Orchestra Bourdon	LP: Victor VIC 1507/TVM 17202/ PVM1-9047/AG 26.41371 CD: Romophone 810 072

Aida, excerpt (Ciel! Mio padre!)

Washington 3 March 1933	Tibbett National SO Kindler	Unpublished radio broadcast
New York 3 December 1933	Tibbett	Unpublished radio broadcast

Aida, excerpt (Pur ti riveggo/Là tra foreste vergine)

Camden NJ 7 February 1924	Martinelli Orchestra Bourdon	Victor VB 73 International Record Collectors Club 126 LP: Victor CBL 100/CDN 5105/ CDN 1006-1007 LP: Pearl GEMM 289 LP: Preiser LV 230/LV 297 LP: Cantilena 6239 CD: Metropolitan Opera MET 706 CD: Memoir CDMOIR 428 CD: Nimbus NI 1777/NI 7805 CD: Romophone 810 062

Aida, excerpt (La fatal pietra)

Camden NJ 8 February 1924	Martinelli Orchestra Bourdon	First version LP: Victor CDN 5105 LP: Cantilena 6239 LP: Pearl GEMM 289 LP: Preiser LV 230 CD: Nimbus NI 1777/NI 7878 CD: Romophone 810 062 Second version Victor ABHB 3 CD: Romophone 810 062
Camden NJ 17 May 1926	Martinelli Orchestra & Chorus Bourdon	Victor 1744/3040 HMV DA 810 45: Victor WCT 6 LP: Victor LCT 1004 LP: Preiser LV 297 CD: Nimbus NI 1777/NI 7846 CD: Metropolitan Opera MET 503 CD: Memoir CDMOIR 428 CD: Romophone 810 072

Aida, excerpt (O terra addio!)

New York 14 January 1920	Hackett Orchestra Romani	Columbia 49734/71000D/9010M LP: Scala (USA) 803 LP: Ember GVC 9 LP: Columbia Y 31150 CD: Pearl GEMMCDS 9964 GVC 9 incorrectly dated December 1920
Camden NJ 8 February 1924	Martinelli Orchestra Bourdon	Victor ABHB 3 LP: Victor PVM1-9047/AG 26.41371 CD: Nimbus NI 1777/NI 7878 CD: Romophone 810 062 PVM1-9047 dated 17 May 1926
Camden NJ 17 May 1926	Baker, Martinelli Orchestra Bourdon	Victor 1745/3041 HMV DA 809 45: Victor WCT 6 LP: Victor LCT 1004 LP: Pearl GEMM 207 CD: Nimbus NI 1777/NI 7846 CD: Metropolitan Opera MET 503 CD: Memoir CDMOIR 428 CD: Romophone 810 072

This Theatre, when filled to its capacity, can be emptied in five minutes. Choose the nearest exit now and in case of need walk quietly (do not run) to that exit in order to avoid panic.

METROPOLITAN OPERA HOUSE

GRAND OPERA SEASON 1918-1919

GIULIO GATTI-CASAZZA, General Manager

SATURDAY AFTERNOON, DECEMBER 21ST, AT 2 O'CLOCK

LA FORZA DEL DESTINO

(THE FORCE OF DESTINY)

OPERA IN FOUR ACTS AND EIGHT TABLEUX

BOOK BY FRANCESCO MARIA PIAVE

(IN ITALIAN)

MUSIC BY GIUSEPPE VERDI

MARQUIS OF CALATRAVA . . . . GIULIO ROSSI
DONNA LEONORA . . . . ROSA PONSELLE
DON CARLOS OF VARGAS . . . . GIUSEPPE DE LUCA
DON ALVARO . . . . ENRICO CARUSO
PREZIOSILLA . . . . SOPHIE BRASLAU
THE ABBOT . . . . JOSE MARDONES
FATHER MELITONE . . . . THOMAS CHALMERS
CURRA . . . . MARIE MATTFELD
THE ALCADE . . . . PAOLO ANANIAN
TRABUCO . . . . GIORDANO PALTRINIERI
A SURGEON . . . . VINCENZO RESCHIGLIAN

HOST AND HOSTESS OF THE INN, MULATTOES, SERVANTS, SPANISH AND ITALIAN SOLDIERS AND PEASANTS, ITALIAN RECRUITS, MONKS, BEGGARS, ETC.

CONDUCTOR . . . . . . GENNARO PAPI

STAGE DIRECTOR . . . . RICHARD ORDYNSKI
CHORUS MASTER . . . . GIULIO SETTI
TECHNICAL DIRECTOR . . . . EDWARD SIEDLE
STAGE MANAGER . . . . ARMANDO AGNINI
PREMIERE DANSEUSE . . . . ROSINA GALLI
PREMIER DANSEUR . . . . GIUSEPPE BONFIGLIO

PROGRAMME CONTINUED ON NEXT PAGE

FIRE NOTICE.—LOOK AROUND *NOW* AND CHOOSE THE NEAREST EXIT TO YOUR SEAT. IN CASE OF FIRE, WALK (*NOT RUN*) TO *THAT EXIT*. DO *NOT* TRY TO BEAT YOUR NEIGHBOR TO THE STREET. *Thomas J. Drennan, Fire Commissioner*

Metropolitan Opera House

GRAND OPERA SEASON 1921-1922

Giulio Gatti-Casazza, *General Manager*

SATURDAY AFTERNOON, JANUARY 28TH, AT 2 O'CLOCK

ERNANI

OPERA IN FOUR ACTS AND FIVE SCENES

BOOK, FOUNDED ON VICTOR HUGO'S "HERNANI," BY F. M. PIAVE

(IN ITALIAN)

MUSIC BY GIUSEPPE VERDI

ERNANI.......................................GIOVANNI MARTINELLI
DON CARLOS.......................................TITTA RUFFO
DON RUY GOMEZ DE SILVA.......................................JOSE MARDONES
ELVIRA.......................................ROSA PONSELLE
GIOVANNA.......................................MINNIE EGENER
DON RICCARDO.......................................GIORDANO PALTRINIERI
JAGO.......................................VINCENZO RESCHIGLIAN

Incidental Divertissement by

ROSINA GALLI, FLORENCE RUDOLPH, GIUSEPPE BONFIGLIO and CORPS DE BALLET

CONDUCTOR.......................................GENNARO PAPI

STAGE DIRECTOR.......................................SAMUEL THEWMAN
CHORUS MASTER.......................................GIULIO SETTI
TECHNICAL DIRECTOR.......................................EDWARD SIEDLE
STAGE MANAGER.......................................ARMANDO AGNINI

SCENIC PRODUCTION BY JOSEPH URBAN

PROGRAMME CONTINUED ON NEXT PAGE

Ernani, excerpt (Ernani involami!)

New York 9 June 1922	Orchestra Romani	Columbia 98028/68037D/7034M LP: Columbia Y 31150 CD: Nimbus NI 1777/NI 7878 CD: Pearl GEMMCDS 9964 Y 31150 incorrectly dated 13 June 1922
Camden NJ 5 December 1923	Orchestra Bourdon	LP: Ed Smith ANNA 1072 CD: Romophone 810 062
Camden NJ 23 January 1924	Orchestra Bourdon	Victor 6440 LP: Victor CBL 100/CDN 1006-1007 LP: Preiser LV 297 CD: Metropolitan Opera MET 218 CD: Nimbus NI 1777/NI 7805 CD: Romophone 810 062
Camden NJ 16 June 1927	Orchestra Bourdon	CD: Romophone 810 072
Camden NJ 17 January 1928	Orchestra Bourdon	Victor 6875 HMV DB 1275 45: Victor WCT 10 LP: Victor LCT 1006/TVM 17202/ PVM1-9047/AG 26.41371 CD: RCA/BMG GD 87810 CD: Memoir CDMOIR 428 CD: Romophone 810 072

La forza del destino

London 1 June 1931	Role of Leonora Franci, Pertile, Pasero Covent Garden Orchestra & Chorus Serafin	Unpublished radio broadcast Transatlantic broadcast

La forza del destino, excerpt (Pace pace!)

New York 3 April 1918	Romani, piano	LP: Ed Smith EJS 532/ANNA 1037 LP: OASI 621 CD: Eklipse EKRCD 46 Test recording for Columbia
New York 5 July 1920	Orchestra Romani	Columbia 49859/68038D/7033M LP: Scala (USA) 803 LP: Ember GVC 9 LP: Columbia Y 31150 CD: Pearl GEMMCDS 9964 GVC 9 incorrectly dated November 1921; Y 31150 incorrectly dated November 1922
Camden NJ 5 December 1923	Orchestra Bourdon	Victor unpublished
Camden NJ 11 December 1923	Orchestra Bourdon	First version CD: Nimbus NI 1777/NI 7878 CD: Romophone 810 062 Second version CD: Nimbus NI 1777/NI 7878 CD: Romophone 810 062
Camden NJ 23 January 1924	Orchestra Bourdon	Victor 6440 LP: Preiser LV 297 LP: Victor CBL 100/CDN 1006-1007/RL 85177 CD: RCA/BMG 09026 61582 CD: Metropolitan Opera MET 218 CD: Romophone 810 062
New York 1 January 1927	Orchestra Shilkret	Unpublished radio broadcast Ponselle's radio debut

Pace pace!/concluded

Camden NJ 17 January 1928	Orchestra Bourdon	First version Victor 6875 HMV DB 1275 LP: Victor TVM 17202/PVM1-9047/ AG 26.41371 LP: Pearl GEMM 181-182 CD: Memoir CDMOIR 428 CD: Pearl GEMMCD 9351 CD: Romophone 810 072 Second version CD: Romophone 810 072
Camden NJ 13-16 June 1928	Orchestra Bourdon	Victor unpublished
New York 3 December 1928	Orchestra Goossens	Unpublished radio broadcast
New York 23 October 1930		Unpublished radio broadcast

La forza del destino, excerpt (La vergine degli angeli)

New York 2 December 1918	Orchestra & Chorus Romani	Columbia 49558/68038D/8910M Columbia (UK) 7227/7340 LP: Scala (USA) 803 LP: Ember GVC 9 LP: Columbia Y 31150 CD: Nimbus NI 1777/NI 7846 CD: Pearl GEMMCDS 9964 GVC 9 incorrectly dated April 1919; Y 31150 incorrectly dated November 1922
Camden NJ 23 January 1928	Pinza Metropolitan Opera Orchestra & Chorus Setti	Victor 8097 HMV DB 1199 HMV (Ireland) IRX 27 45: Victor WCT 4 LP: Victor LCT 1003/VTM 17202/ CBL 100/CDN 1006-1007 LP: Top Artists' Platter TAP 314 LP: Pearl GEMM 181-182 CD: Metropolitan Opera MET 105 CD: Nimbus NI 1777/NI 7805 CD: Pearl GEMMCD 9351 CD: Memoir CDMOIR 428 CD: Romophone 810 072 CD: BBC Records CD 715
New York 10 December 1936	Orchestra & Chorus Kelsey	LP: OASI 635 CD: Eklipse EKRCD 51
Baltimore 8 May 1953	Pinza Piano accompaniment	LP: Ed Smith EJS 243/ANNA 1037 LP: Collectors Limited Edition MDP 012

La forza del destino, excerpt (Io muoio!/Non imprecare!)

New York 1 January 1928	Martinelli, Pinza Metropolitan Opera Orchestra Setti	Unpublished radio broadcast
Camden NJ 18 January 1928	Martinelli, Pinza Orchestra Bourdon	First version CD: Romophone 810 072 Second version Victor 8104 HMV DB 1202 LP: Victor CBL 100/CDN 1006-1007 LP: HMV CSLP 504 LP: Pearl GEMM 181-182 CD: RCA/BMG GD 87810 CD: Pearl GEMMCD 9351 CD: Memoir CDMOIR 428 CD: Romophone 810 072

Otello, excerpt (Piangea cantando)

Camden NJ 23 January 1924	Orchestra Bourdon	Victor 6474 HMV DB 807 LP: Victor TVM 17202/PVM1-9047/ AG 26.41371 LP: Preiser LV 297 CD: RCA/BMG GD 87810 CD: Nimbus NI 1777/NI 7805 CD: Romophone 810 062

Otello, excerpt (Ave Maria)

New York 6 June 1922	Orchestra Romani	Columbia 98029/68060D/7063M LP: Scala (USA) 851 LP: Columbia Y 31150 CD: Pearl GEMMCDS 9964 Y 31150 incorrectly dated 12 June 1922
Camden NJ 23 December 1924	Orchestra Bourdon	Victor 6474 HMV DB 807 LP: Victor PVM1-9047/AG 26.41371 LP: Preiser LV 297 CD: Nimbus NI 1777/NI 7805 CD: Romophone 810 062 PVM1-9047 incorrectly dated January 1924
New York 27 September 1936	Orchestra Rapee	LP: Ed Smith EJS 184/EJS 190/ UORC 118/ANNA 1036 LP: Collectors Limited Edition MDP 012

La traviata

London 9 June 1931	Role of Violetta Borgioli, Noble Covent Garden Orchestra & Chorus Serafin	Unpublished radio broadcast Transatlantic broadcast
New York 5 January 1935	Jagel, Tibbett Metropolitan Opera Orchestra & Chorus Panizza	LP: Ed Smith EJS 107/MOP 2 LP: Pearl GEMM 235-236 CD: Pearl GEMMCDS 9317 Excerpts LP: Ed Smith EJS 190/ANNA 1036

La traviata, excerpt (Parigi o cara)

New York 19 January 1933	Borgioli Harlem PO	Unpublished radio broadcast

La traviata, excerpt (Addio del passato)

New York 7 December 1930	Orchestra Pasternack	Unpublished radio broadcast
New York 11 December 1934		Unpublished radio broadcast
New York 9 April 1934		Unpublished radio broadcast
Los Angeles 24 May 1936	Los Angeles PO Rapee	LP: Ed Smith EJS 104/EJS 190 LP: Collectors Limited Edition MDP 012

Il trovatore

New York 16 January 1932	Role of Leonora Petrova, Lauri-Volpi, Danise, Pasero Metropolitan Opera Orchestra & Chorus Bellezza	Unpublished Met broadcast Complete opera may not have been broadcast

Il trovatore, excerpt (Mira d'acerbe lagrime)

New York 30 December 1920	Stracciari Orchestra Romani	Columbia 49922/71000D/9010M LP: Scala (USA) 838 LP: Columbia Y 31150 LP: Pearl GEMM 181-182 CD: Metropolitan Opera MET 218 CD: Memoir CDMOIR 428 CD: Pearl GEMMCDS 9964

Il trovatore, excerpt (Tacea la notte placida)

New York 16 November 1922	Orchestra Romani	Columbia 98051/68036D/7033M LP: Scala (USA) 851 LP: Ed Smith ANNA 1072 LP: Columbia Y 31150 LP: Pearl GEMM 181-182 CD: Nimbus NI 1777/NI 7878 CD: Pearl GEMMCDS 9964
New York 10 April 1930		Unpublished radio broadcast

Il trovatore, excerpt (D'amor sull' ali rosee)

New York 10 December 1918	Orchestra Romani	Columbia 49559/68058D/8909M LP: Scala (USA) 803 LP: Ember GVC 9 LP: Pearl GEMM 181-182 CD: Metropolitan Opera MET 409 CD: Nimbus NI 1777/NI 7846 CD: Memoir CDMOIR 428 CD: Pearl GEMMCDS 9964 GVC 9 incorrectly dated September 1919; Y 31150 incorrectly dated February 1923

Il trovatore, excerpt (Miserere)

New York 1 January 1928	Martinelli Metropolitan Opera Orchestra & Chorus Setti	Unpublished radio broadcast
Camden NJ 23 January 1928	Martinelli Metropolitan Opera Orchestra & Chorus Setti	First version Victor 8097 HMV (Ireland) IRX 27 LP: Victor PVM1-9047/AG 26.41371/ VL 42799 LP: Pearl GEMM 181-182/GEMM 207 CD: Memoir CDMOIR 428 CD: Romophone 810 072 Second version Victor 8097 HMV DB 1199 CD: Romophone 810 072

I vespri siciliani, excerpt (Mercè dilette amiche)

New York 4 November 1919	Orchestra Romani	Columbia 49686/68037D LP: Scala (USA) 838 LP: Columbia Y 31150 CD: Metropolitan Opera MET 218 CD: Pearl GEMMCDS 9964 Y 31150 incorrectly dated 13 June 1922
New York 13 October 1929	Orchestra Pasternack	Unpublished radio broadcast
New York 7 December 1930	Orchestra Pasternack	Unpublished radio broadcast
New York 18 October 1931	Orchestra Pasternack	Unpublished radio broadcast
New York 19 March 1933		Unpublished radio broadcast

VUILLERMOZ

Jardin d'amour

Baltimore 5 September 1953		Unpublished private recording

RICHARD WAGNER (1813-1883)

Lohengrin, excerpt (Einsam in trüben Tagen)

New York 21 September 1923	Orchestra Romani	Columbia AF 1 LP: Scala (USA) 838 CD: Nimbus NI 1777/NI 7846 CD: Legato BIM 701 CD: Pearl GEMMCDS 9964

Tristan und Isolde, excerpt (Mild und leise)

Baltimore 6 September 1953		LP: Ed Smith EJS 243 LP: Collectors Limited Edition MDP 036

Träume/Wesendonk-Lieder

Baltimore 19 October 1954	Chicagov, piano	LP: Ed Smith ASCO 125 CD: Romophone 810 222

VINCENT WALLACE (1812-1865)

Maritana, excerpt (Scenes that are brightest)

New York 9 September 1921	Orchestra Romani	Columbia 49982/68078D/7062M LP: Scala (USA) 803 LP: Ember GVC 9 CD: Metropolitan Opera MET 218 CD: Pearl GEMMCDS 9964 GVC 9 incorrectly dated March 1922

WENRICH

On moonlight bay

New York 10 December 1936	Orchestra Kelsey	CD: Eklipse EKRCD 46/EKRCD 51

ERMANNO WOLF-FERRARI (1876-1948)

Rispetto

New York 19 January 1933	Harlem PO	Unpublished radio broadcast
New York 11 December 1933		Unpublished radio broadcast
Baltimore 6 March 1953		Unpublished private recording
Baltimore 20 October 1954	Chicagov, piano	First version CD: Romophone 810 222 Second version LP: Victor LM 1889/L 16493 CD: Romophone 810 222

ADDITIONAL POPULAR MATERIAL RECORDED BY PONSELLE

As I pass by

New York 8 October 1934		Unpublished radio broadcast

Auld lang syne

New York 12 March 1933		Unpublished radio broadcast
New York 1935	Crooks, Melchior, Tibbett	Unpublished radio broadcast

Because I love you dearly

New York 10 December 1934		Unpublished radio broadcast

Carmen-Carmela, arranged by Ross

Baltimore 21 October 1954	Chicagov, piano	LP: Victor LM 2047 CD: RCA/BMG GD 87810 CD: Romophone 810 2222

Comin' thro' the rye

New York 9 December 1919	C.Ponselle Orchestra Romani	Columbia 78847/36002D LP: Scala (USA) 838 CD: Metropolitan Opera MET 218 CD: Pearl GEMMCDS 9964
New York 11 March 1936	Orchestra Kostelanetz	LP: Ed Smith EJS 192
Baltimore 22 July 1951	C.Ponselle	Private acetate recording

Unpublished radio broadcasts of the song dated 27 March 1932, 19 March 1933, 9 April 1934 and 10 December 1934 may also survive

The cuckoo clock

New York 1 October 1934	Orchestra Kostelanetz	LP: Ed Smith EJS 192 CD: Vocal Archives VA 1120

Unpublished radio broadcasts of the song dated 27 November 1932, 15 November 1933, 24 December 1933, 4 June 1934, 5 November 1934 and 1 April 1936 may also survive

Danny Boy, arranged by Weatherly

New York 4 March 1936	Orchestra Kostelanetz	LP: Ed Smith EJS 192 LP: Collectors Limited Edition MDP 012

Drink to me only

Baltimore 19 October	Chicagov, piano	LP: Victor LM 1889/L 16493 CD: Romophone 810 2222

Unpublished radio broadcasts of the song dated 19 February 1933 and 15 November 1933 may also survive

Estrellita

New York 19 November 1934		Unpublished radio broadcast

La golondrina, arranged by Serradell

New York 15 October 1934	Orchestra Kostelanetz	LP: Ed Smith EJS 532

Go to sleep my dusky baby

New York 18 March 1936		Unpublished radio broadcast

Gypsy love song/Russian gypsy song

New York 9 June 1934		Unpublished radio broadcast
Baltimore 16 October 1952		Unpublished private recording
Baltimore 30 March 1957		LP: Ponselle by Request RPX 102 LP: Collectors Limited Edition MDP 036

He will come to me

New York 22 January 1933		Unpublished radio broadcast

In the gloaming

New York 12 November 1934		Unpublished radio broadcast

Jeune fillette, arranged by Weckerlin

Baltimore 17 October 1954	Chicagov, piano	LP: Victor LM 2047 CD: Romophone 810 2222

Little man you've had a busy day

New York 4 June 1934		Unpublished radio broadcast

Love's old sweet song

New York 7 May 1934		Unpublished radio broadcast

O come all ye faithful

New York 24 December 1933-1934		Unpublished radio broadcast

O holy night

Baltimore 25 December 1952		Private acetate recording

The sleigh

New York 19 November 1934		Unpublished radio broadcast

Star vicino, attributed to Rosa

Baltimore 15 April 1950		Private acetate recording
Baltimore 19 October 1954	Chicagov, piano	LP: Victor LM 2047 CD: Romophone 810 2222

Sylvelin

New York 22 October 1934		Unpublished radio broadcast

Vieni sul mar

New York 24 December 1934		Unpublished radio broadcast

Violetera

New York 29 October 1934		Unpublished radio broadcast

Will o' the wisp

New York
15 October
1934

Unpublished radio broadcast

You tell it to her

New York
27 October
1934

Unpublished radio broadcast

SELECTED INTERVIEW MATERIAL

Ponselle discusses the role of Norma with Boris Goldowsky

Baltimore 17 March 1954	CD: Eklipse EKRCD 51

Ponselle discusses the role of Leonora in La forza del destino

Baltimore 11 March 1960	CD: Eklipse EKRCD 51

Spoken comments on the songs contained in Victor LM 1889

Baltimore 16-20 October 1954	CD: Romophone 810 2222

Ponselle recalls her first Columbia recordings and her 1918 Met début

New York December 1971	LP: Columbia (USA) Y 31150

Eleanor Steber
1914-1990

with additional assistance from Michael Gray

Discography compiled
by John Hunt

ADOLPHE ADAM (1803-1856)

Cantique Noël

New York December 1977	Stony Baroque Players	LP: Steber Music Foundation ESMF 4-5

JOHANN SEBASTIAN BACH (1685-1750)

Mass in B minor

Philadelphia 25-26 April 1962	Elias, Verreau, Cross Temple University Choir Philadelphia Orchestra Ormandy	LP: Columbia M3L 280/M3S 680 LP: CBS BRG 72114-72115/ SBRG 72114-72115

Cantata No 51 "Jauchzet Gott in allen Landen"

Syracuse NY 1962	I.Kipnis ensemble I.Kipnis	LP: Private issue SLS 7416

Cantata No 21, excerpt (Seufzen, Weinen)

New York 20 September 1951	Columbia SO Rudolf <u>Sung in English</u>	LP: Columbia ML 4521/ML 5226/P 14171 CD: Sony MHK 62356

Cantata No 68, excerpt (Mein gläubiges Herze)

New York 20 September 1951	Columbia SO Rudolf <u>Sung in English</u>	LP: Columbia ML 4521/ML 5226/P 14171 CD: Sony MHK 62356

Ave Maria, arranged by Gounod

New York 31 March-14 April 1941	Biltcliffe, organ	LP: Private issue SLP 404

ALFRED BACHELET (1864-1944)

Chère nuit

New York 5 May 1941	Quillan, piano	78: Victor 18088 CD: RCA/BMG GD 60521
Boston 20 April 1975	Rogers, piano	LP: Steber Music Foundation ESMF 2

ERNST BACON (Born 1898)

4 poems by Emily Dickinson

Date not confirmed	Biltcliffe, piano	LP: Private issue SLP 411-412/ SLPS 7411-7412 LP: Desto D 411-412

MARY BAKER EDDY

4 songs from the Christian Science songbook

Boston Date not confirmed	McDonald, organ	LP: Private issue SLP 402/SLP 410
Boston Date not confirmed	McDonald, organ Sung in German	LP: Private issue SLP 403/SLP 410
Boston Date not confirmed	McDonald, organ Sung in French	LP: Private issue SLP 409/SLP 410

SAMUEL BARBER (1910-1981)

Vanessa

New York 1 February 1958	Role of Vanessa Elias, Resnik, Gedda, Nagy, Cehanovsky, Tozzi Metropolitan Opera Orchestra & Chorus Mitropoulos	Unpublished Met broadcast
New York 23 February- 10 April 1958	Elias, Resnik, Gedda, Nagy, Cehanovsky, Tozzi Metropolitan Opera Orchestra & Chorus Mitropoulos	LP: Victor LM 6138/LSC 6138/ ARL2-2094/RL 02094 CD: RCA/BMG RG 78992/GD 87899 Excerpts LP: Victor LM 6062/LSC 6062/ SP 33-21/RL 85177 CD: RCA/BMG 09026 626982 ARL2-2094 and RL 02094 omitted dialogue

Vanessa, excerpt (To leave, to break)

New York 16 April 1966	Dunn, Thebom, J.Alexander, Harvuot Metropolitan Opera Orchestra Adler	LP: MRF Records MRF 7 Gala farewell performance in old Metropolitan opera house

Knoxville, Summer of 1915

New York 7 November 1950	Dumbarton Oaks Chamber Orchestra Strickland	LP: Columbia ML 2174/ML 5843/ 3216 0230 CD: Sony MPK 46727
New York 10 October 1958	Biltcliffe, piano	CD: VAI Audio VAIA 10052
Trenton NJ 13 January 1962	Trenton SO Harsanyi	LP: Private issue SLS 7420

Nuovoletta

Date not confirmed	Biltcliffe, piano	LP: Private issue SLP 411-412/ SLPS 7411-7412 LP: Desto D 411-412

JOSEPH BARNBY (1838-1896)

Now the day is over

Date not confirmed	Biltcliffe, piano	LP: Private issue SLP 404

LUDWIG VAN BEETHOVEN (1770-1827)

Fidelio

New York 10-17 December 1944	Role of Marzelline Bampton, Peerce, Laderoute, Belarsky, Janssen, Moscona NBC SO and Chorus Toscanini	LP: Victor LM 6025/AT 204/VCM 9/ AT 1099-1100 LP: HMV ALP 1304-1305 CD: RCA/BMG GD 60273

Missa solemnis

New York 1948	Merriman, Hain, Alvary Westminster Choir NYPSO Walter	CD: AS-Disc AS 301
New York 8 November 1953	Tangeman, Smith-Spence, Harrell Westminster Choir NYPSO Mitropoulos	LP: Melodram MEL 233

Ah perfido!, concert aria

Philadelphia 15 November 1953	Philadelphia Orchestra Ormandy	Columbia unpublished
Cleveland 5 May 1970	Cleveland Orchestra Levine	CD: VAI Audio VAIA 10122

An die ferne Geliebte, song cycle

Syracuse NY 1962	Biltcliffe, piano	LP: Private issue SLP 417

Lieder: Die Ehre Gottes; Andenken; Wonne der Wehmut

Syracuse NY 1962	Biltcliffe, piano	LP: Private issue SLP 417

VINCENZO BELLINI (1801-1835)

I puritani, excerpt (Qui la voce)

New York 10 October 1958	Biltcliffe, piano	LP: Private issue SLP 101 CD: Legato BIM 712 CD: VAI Audio VAIA 10052

BENNARD

The old rugged cross

New York 19 December 1947	Harshaw Victor Orchestra Case	78: Victor 10-1449 45: Victor 49-0569

ALBAN BERG (1885-1935)

Wozzeck

New York 14 March 1959	Role of Marie Roggero, Baum, Anthony, Uhde, Dönch Metropolitan Opera Orchestra & Chorus Böhm	Unpublished Met broadcast
New York 8 April 1961	Roggero, Baum, Anthony, Uhde, Herbert Metropolitan Opera Orchestra & Chorus Böhm	Unpublished Met broadcast

7 frühe Lieder

Syracuse NY 1962	Biltcliffe, piano	LP: Private issue SLP 417

WILLIAM BERGSMA (1921-1994)

Lullee lullay

Date not confirmed	Biltcliffe, piano	LP: Private issue SLP 411-412/ SLPS 7411-7412 LP: Desto D 411-412

IRVING BERLIN (1888-1989)

White Christmas

New York 20 December 1954	Firestone Orchestra	VHS Video: Bel Canto Society 69113

HECTOR BERLIOZ (1803-1869)

Les troyens

New York 29 December 1959	Role of Dido Resnik, Sarfaty, Cassilly, Singher American Opera Society Orchestra and Chorus Lawrence	CD: VAI Audio VAIA 10062

Les nuits d'été

Atlanta GA 5 April 1953	NYPSO Mitropoulos	CD: AS-Disc AS 619
New York 21 January 1954	Columbia SO Mitropoulos	LP: Columbia ML 4940/ML 5843 LP: Philips NBL 5029/N02115L CD: Sony MHK 62356
New York 10 October 1958	Biltcliffe, piano	CD: VAI Audio VAIA 10052 This performance omits Les lagunes

La captive

New York 19 May 1954	Columbia SO Morel	LP: Columbia ML 4940 LP: Philips NBL 5029/N02115L CD: Sony MHK 62356

Le jeune pâtre breton

New York 19 May 1954	Columbia SO Morel	LP: Columbia ML 4940 LP: Philips NBL 5029/N02115L CD: Sony MHK 62356

Zaide

New York 19 May 1954	Columbia SO Morel	LP: Columbia ML 4940 LP: Philips NBL 5029/N02115L CD: Sony MHK 62356
Boston 20 April 1975	Rogers, piano	LP: Steber Music Foundation ESMF 2

EDWIN BILTCLIFFE

Song

New York 10 October 1958	Biltcliffe, piano	LP: Private issue SLP 101 CD: VAI Audio VAIA 10052

GEORGES BIZET (1838-1875)

Carmen, excerpt (Je dis que rien ne m'épouvante)

New York May 1940	Metropolitan Opera Orchestra Pelletier	78: World's Greatest Music series LP: Victor CAL 221/CFL 101 78 edition published without artists' names
New York 26 June 1941	Victor Orchestra O'Connell	Victor unpublished
London 17 September 1947	Philharmonia Susskind	78: Victor 12-0690 78: HMV DB 6514 LP: EMI EX 769 7411 CD: EMI CHS 769 7412 CD: RCA/BMG GD 60251 CD: International Record Collector IRCC 809 CD: Metropolitan Opera Guild CD 211

JAMES BLAND (1854-1911)

Carry me back to old Virginny

New York 13 February 1950	Firestone Orchestra	CD: VAI Audio VAIA 10722 VHS Video: Bel Canto Society 69112

JOHANNES BRAHMS (1833-1897)

Ein deutsches Requiem

New York 3-6 December 1947	Pease Victor Orchestra Shaw Chorale Shaw	78: Victor M 1236 45: Victor WDM 1236 LP: Victor LM 6004

Geistliches Wiegenlied

New York December 1977	Walevska, cello Biltcliffe, piano	LP: Steber Music Foundation ESMF 4-5

BENJAMIN BRITTEN (1913-1976)

Winter words

New York 7 December 1974	Biltcliffe, piano	LP: Steber Music Foundation ESMF 2

NACIO BROWN (1896-1964)

Love is where you find it

New York 17 September 1951	Firestone Orchestra Barlow	VHS Video: Bel Canto Society 69102

HENRY BURLEIGH (1866-1949)

The trees have grown so

New York 31 March 1941	Quillan, piano	Victor unpublished

CHARLES CADMAN (1881-1946)

At dawning

Date not confirmed	Vann, piano	LP: Private issue SLS 7413

JOSEPH CANTELOUBE (1879-1957)

Chants d'Auvergne: Passo pel prat; Berceuse; Tibilou par una sera

New York 1956	Biltcliffe, piano	CD: VAI Audio VAIA 10052

HOAGY CARMICHAEL (1899-1981)

Stardust

New York 25 February 1946	Victor Orchestra Blackstone	78: Victor 11-9186
New York 26 June 1950	Firestone Orchestra	VHS Video: Bel Canto Society 69134

GUSTAVE CHARPENTIER (1860-1950)

Louise, excerpt (Depuis le jour)

London 17 September 1947	Philharmonia Susskind	78: Victor 12-0690 78: HMV DB 6514 CD: RCA/BMG GD 60521 CD: Metropolitan Opera Guild CD 211
New York 14 November 1949	Firestone Orchestra Barlow	VHS Video: Bel Canto Society 69102
New York 10 October 1958	Biltcliffe, piano	CD: VAI Audio VAIA 10052
New York 4 October 1973	Biltcliffe, piano	LP: RCA ARL1-0436

PIETRO CIMARA (1887-1967)

Canto di primavera

New York 2-14 April 1941	Quillan, piano	78: Victor 10-1099

ERIC COATES (1886-1957)

Birdsong at eventide

New York 9 December 1949	Firestone Orchestra Barlow	78: Columbia MM 906 45: Columbia A 906 LP: Columbia ML 2105

AARON COPLAND (1900-1990)

Old American songs: Long time ago; Simple gifts

New York 1956	Biltcliffe, piano	CD: VAI Audio VAIA 10052

NOEL COWARD (1899-1973)

I'll see you again

New York 20 March 1950	Firestone Orchestra	VHS Video: Bel Canto Society 69134

CRAPSEY-SACCO

Rapunzel

New York 31 March-14 April 1941	Quillan, piano	78: Victor 10-1071

REGINALD DE KOVEN (1859-1920)

O promise me!

Date not confirmed	Vann, piano	LP: Private issue SLS 7413

CLAUDE DEBUSSY (1862-1918)

L'enfant prodigue, excerpt (Air de Lia)

New York 5 October 1938	Piano accompaniment	CD: VAI Audio VAIA 10722

Chevaux de bois

Boston 20 April 1975	Rogers, piano	LP: Steber Music Foundation ESMF 2

CARL VON DITTERSDORF (1739-1799)

Arcifanfano re de' matti

New York 1965	Role of Gloriosa Russell, D.Smith, Brooks, McCollum, Rehfuss Clarion Music Society Jenkins	CD: VAI Audio VAIA 10102

GAETONO DONIZETTI (1797-1848)

Lucia di Lammermoor, excerpt (Chi me frema)

New York 30 November 1953	Stevens, Sullivan, Rounseville, Thomas, Hines Firestone Orchestra	LP: Legendary LR 141 VHS Video: Bel Canto Society 69112

ESMF

ESMF 1

THE ELEANOR STEBER MUSIC FOUNDATION
PRESENTS

To Clifford Elkin

STEBER IN RECITAL

Cordial greetings –
Eleanor Steber

December 7, 1974
Edwin Biltcliffe, Assisting Artist
Church of St. Paul and St. Andrew, New York
34th Anniversary, Metropolitan Opera Debut

April 20, 1975
Allen Rogers, Assisting Artist
Jordan Hall, New England Conservatory of Music
Opening Weekend, Bicentennial Year, Boston

FULL-LENGTH OPERAS
produced by the
METROPOLITAN OPERA ASSOCIATION
offered exclusively on Columbia Records
Uninterrupted listening pleasure is yours. Now, you can enjoy these brilliant productions—highlights of any Metropolitan Season—all year around on Columbia Records. All are full-length operas.
Mozart: Cosi Fan Tutte (Women Are Like That) (Sung in English). Eleanor Steber, Soprano; Richard Tucker, Tenor; Frank Guarrera, Baritone; Blanche Thebom, Mezzo-Soprano; Roberta Peters, Soprano, and others, Fritz Stiedry conducting Set SL-122
Leoncavallo: Pagliacci (Sung in Italian). Lucine Amara, Soprano; Richard Tucker, Tenor; Giuseppe Valdengo, Baritone, and others, Fausto Cleva conducting Set SL-113
The Metropolitan Opera Version of Johann Strauss' Fledermaus (Sung in English). Lily Pons, Soprano; Ljuba Welitch, Soprano; Richard Tucker, Tenor; Charles Kullman, Tenor, and others, Eugene Ormandy conducting Set SL-108
Puccini: La Bohème (Sung in Italian). Bidú Sayão, Soprano; Richard Tucker, Tenor; Salvatore Baccaloni, Basso, and others, Giuseppe Antonicelli, conducting Set SL-101
Puccini: Madame Butterfly (Sung in Italian). Eleanor Steber, Soprano; Richard Tucker, Tenor; Giuseppe Valdengo, Baritone; Jean Madeira, Mezzo-Soprano, and others, Max Rudolf conducting Set SL-104
Gounod: Faust (Sung in French). Eleanor Steber, Soprano; Eugene Conley, Tenor; Cesare Siepi, Bass; Frank Guarrera, Baritone, and others, Fausto Cleva conducting Set SL-112
Humperdinck: Hansel and Gretel (Sung in English). Risë Stevens, Mezzo-Soprano; Nadine Conner, Soprano; Thelma Votipka, Soprano; John Brownlee, Baritone, and others, Max Rudolf conducting Set SL-102
This is a list you should hold on to. Wouldn't it be a good idea to take it with you the next time you visit your record dealer?
Up to a full hour of music on a single record
Unequalled in sound reproduction and durable quality, each Columbia "Lp" is a superb, lasting recording of great music—sung and played by the world's greatest artists.
COLUMBIA LP MASTERWORKS

HENRI DUPARC (1848-1933)

Chanson triste

New York 5 May 1941	Quillan, piano	78: Victor 18088 CD: RCA/BMG GD 60521
Date not confirmed	Rogers, piano	LP: Steber Music Foundation ESMF 2

ANTONIN DVORAK (1841-1904)

Songs my mother taught me

New York 24 December 1947	Russ Case Orchestra	78: Victor M 1243

SAMMY FAIN (1902-1989)

I'll be seeing you

New York 9 December 1949	Firestone Orchestra Barlow	78: Columbia MM 906 45: Columbia A 906 LP: Columbia ML 2105
New York 6 August 1951	Firestone Orchestra	VHS Video: Bel Canto Society 69134

GABRIEL FAURE (1845-1924)

Nell

Boston 20 April 1975	Rogers, piano	LP: Steber Music Foundation ESMF 2

JOHN FEARIS (Born 1867)

Beautiful isle of somewhere

New York 19 December 1947	Harshaw Victor Orchestra Case	78: Victor 10-1449 45: Victor 49-0569

FIELDS

You kissed me

New York 20 March 1950	Firestone Orchestra	VHS Video: Bel Canto Society 69134

IDABELLE FIRESTONE

If I could tell you

New York 10 December 1947	Russ Case Orchestra	78: Victor M 1243
New York 24 May 1948	Firestone Orchestra	LP: Legendary LR 141
New York 5 December 1949	Warren Firestone Orchestra Barlow	VHS Video: Bel Canto Society 69110
New York 26 June 1950	Firestone Orchestra	VHS Video: Bel Canto Society 69134
New York 25 December 1950	Firestone Orchestra Barlow	VHS Video: Bel Canto Society 69113
New York 28 May 1951	Firestone Orchestra	VHS Video: Bel Canto Society 69112
New York 2 November 1953	Firestone Orchestra	VHS Video: Bel Canto Society 69122

In my garden

New York 1943	Firestone Orchestra	LP: Legendary LR 141
New York 10 December 1947	Russ Case Orchestra	78: Victor M 1243
New York 5 December 1949	Warren Firestone Orchestra Barlow	VHS Video: Bel Canto Society 69110
New York 13 February 1950	Firestone Orchestra	VHS Video: Bel Canto Society 69122
New York 27 October 1952	Firestone Orchestra	VHS Video: Bel Canto Society 69134
New York 30 November 1953	Firestone Orchestra	VHS Video: Bel Canto Society 69112
New York 23 December 1957	Firestone Orchestra Barlow	VHS Video: Bel Canto Society 69113

You are the song in my heart

New York 13 February 1950	Firestone Orchestra	VHS Video: Bel canto Society 69134
New York 28 May 1951	Firestone Orchestra	VHS Video: Bel Canto Society 69112

FRIEDRICH VON FLOTOW (1812-1883)

Martha, excerpt (Last rose of summer)

New York 21 October 1946	Firestone Orchestra Barlow	CD: VAI Audio VAIA 10722

HENRY GEEHL (1881-1961)

For you alone

New York 9 June 1952	Firestone Orchestra Barlow	VHS Video: Bel Canto Society 69102

GEORGE GERSHWIN (1898-1937)

Porgy and Bess, excerpt (Summertime)

New York 25 February 1946	Victor Orchestra Blackton	78: Victor 11-9186 LP: HMV CSLP 504 LP: Readers' Digest RDA 49A LP: RCA ARL2-2094
New York 2 August 1954	Firestone Orchestra	VHS Video: Bel Canto Society 69112

CHARLES GOUNOD (1818-1893)

Faust

New York 21-25 May 1951	Role of Marguérite Roggero, Votipka, Conley, Siepi, Guarrera Metropolitan Opera Orchestra & Chorus Cleva	LP: Columbia SL 112/Y3-32103 LP: Philips ABL 3096-3098 LP: CBS 77360

Faust, excerpts (Il était un roi de Thulé; Ah je ris!)

New York 19 September 1946	Victor Orchestra Morel	78: Victor 11-9838 45: Victor 49-0289 CD: RCA/BMG GD 60521

Faust, excerpt (Ainsi que la brise)

New York 31 May 1940	Jobin, Cordon Metropolitan Opera Orchestra & Chorus Pelletier	78: World's Greatest Music SR 49-50 LP: Victor CAL 221/CFL 101 CD: VAI Audio VAIA 10232 78 edition published without artists' names

Faust, excerpt (Il se fait tard)

Philadelphia 17 June 1940	Tokatayan Philadelphia Orchestra Pelletier	78: World's Greatest Music SR 49-50 LP: Victor CAL 221/CFL 101 CD: VAI Audio VAIA 10232 78 edition published without artists' names

Faust, excerpt (Alerte! alerte!)

Philadelphia 17 June 1940	Tokatayan, Cordon Philadelphia Orchestra Pelletier	78: World's Greatest Music SR 49-50 LP: Victor CAL 221/CFL 101 CD: VAI Audio VAIA 10232 78 edition published without artists' names
New York 30 November 1953	Sullivan, Hines Firestone Orchestra	LP: Legendary LR 141 VHS Video: Bel Canto Society 69112

Roméo et Juliette, excerpt (Je veux vivre dans cette rêve)

New York 19 September 1946	Victor Orchestra Morel	78: Victor 12-0526 CD: RCA/BMG GD 60521

MAURICE GREENE (1696-1755)

Sing me to sleep

New York 9 December 1949	Firestone Orchestra Barlow	78: Columbia MM 906 45: Columbia A 906 LP: Columbia ML 2105
Date not confirmed	Vann, piano	LP: Private issue SLS 7413

CHARLES GRIFFES (1884-1920)

By a lonely forest pathway

New York 31 March- 14 April 1941	Quillan, piano	78: Victor 10-1071

Waikiki

Date not confirmed	Biltcliffe, piano	LP: Private issue SLP 411-412/ SLPS 7411-7412 LP: Desto D 411-412

FRANZ XAVER GRUBER (1787-1863)

Stille Nacht heilige Nacht

New York 22 December 1947	Firestone Orchestra Sung in English	LP: Legendary LR 136
New York 25 December 1950	Firestone Orchestra Barlow	VHS Video: Bel Canto Society 69113

RICHARD HAGEMAN (1882-1966)

Christ went up into the hills

Date not confirmed	Biltcliffe, organ	LP: Private issue SLP 404

At the well

New York 31 March 1941	Quillan, piano	Victor unpublished

GEORGE FRIDERIC HANDEL (1685-1759)

Messiah, excerpt (I know that my redeemer liveth)

Philadelphia 8 June 1942	Victor Orchestra O'Connell	78: Victor M 927
New York 18 September 1951	Columbia SO Rudolf	LP: Columbia ML 4521/ML 5226 /P 14171 CD: Sony MHK 62356 CD: Metropolitan Opera MET 208
New York 12 April 1954	Firestone Orchestra	VHS Video: Bel Canto Society 69122

Messiah, excerpt (Rejoice greatly!)

Philadelphia 8 June 1942	Victor Orchestra O'Connell	78: Victor M 927
Boston 20 April 1975	Rogers, piano	LP: Steber Music Foundation ESMF 1
New York December 1977	Stony Baroque Players	LP: Steber Music Foundation ESMF 4-5

Messiah, excerpt (He shall feed his flock)

New York December 1977	Stony Baroque Players	LP: Steber Music Foundation ESMF 4-5

Alexander's Feast, excerpt (With artful beguiling)

Boston 20 April 1975	Rogers, piano	LP: Steber Music Foundation ESMF 1

Giulio Cesare, excerpt (Se pietà di me non senti)

Boston 20 April 1975	Rogers, piano	LP: Steber Music Foundation ESMF 1

CLIFFORD HARKER

God shall wipe away all tears

Date not confirmed	Biltcliffe, organ	LP: Private issue SLP 404

ANNIE HARRISON (1851-1944)

In the gloaming

New York 24 December 1947	Russ Case Orchestra	78: Victor M 1243

THOMAS HASTINGS (1784-1872)

Rock of ages

Date not confirmed	Biltcliffe, organ	LP: Private issue SLP 404

HAWTHORNE

Whispering hope

New York 19 December 1947	Harshaw Victor Orchestra Case	78: Victor 10-1463 45: Victor 49-1026

FRANZ JOSEF HAYDN (1732-1809)

Die Schöpfung, excerpt (Es beut die Flur)

Philadelphia 8 June 1942	Victor Orchestra O'Connell Sung in English	78: Victor M 927
New York 18 September 1951	Columbia SO Rudolf Sung in English	LP: Columbia ML 4521/P 14171 CD: Sony MHK 62356

Die Schöpfung, excerpt (Auf starkem Fittiche)

Philadelphia 8 June 1942	Victor Orchestra O'Connell Sung in English	Victor unpublished

Die Jahreszeiten, excerpt (Welche Labung für die Sinne)

New York 22 February 1945	Victor Orchestra Leinsdorf Sung in English	Victor unpublished

Die Jahreszeiten, excerpt (Willkommen jetzt, o dunkler Hain!)

New York 5 September 1945	Victor Orchestra Leinsdorf Sung in English	Victor unpublished

VICTOR HERBERT (1859-1924)

Ah sweet mystery of life

New York 14 March 1951	Percy Faith Orchestra	45: Columbia A 1011 LP: Columbia ML 2192/P6-1503

I'm falling in love with someone

New York 14 November 1949	Firestone Orchestra Barlow	VHS Video: Bel Canto Society 69102
New York 16 March 1951	Percy Faith Orchestra	45: Columbia A 1011 LP: Columbia ML 2192

Italian street song

New York 14 November 1949	Firestone Orchestra Barlow	VHS Video: Bel Canto Society 69102
New York 16 March 1951	Percy Faith Orchestra	45: Columbia A 1011 LP: Columbia ML 2192

Kiss in the dark

New York 3 January 1946	Firestone Orchestra	LP: Legendary LR 141
New York 16 March 1951	Percy Faith Orchestra	45: Columbia A 1011 LP: Columbia ML 2192
New York 17 September 1951	Firestone Orchestra Barlow	VHS Video: Bel Canto Society 69102

Kiss me again

New York 14 March 1951	Percy Faith Orchestra	45: Columbia A 1011 LP: Columbia ML 2192

Sweethearts

New York 16 March 1951	Percy Faith Orchestra	45: Columbia A 1011 LP: Columbia ML 2192/P6-1503
New York 9 June 1952	Firestone Orchestra Barlow	VHS Video: Bel Canto Society 69102

Thine alone

New York 14 March 1951	Percy Faith Orchestra	45: Columbia A 1011 LP: Columbia ML 2192

Toyland

New York 20 December 1954	Firestone Orchestra Pelletier	VHS Video: Bel Canto Society 69113

When you're away

New York 14 March 1951	Percy Faith Orchestra	45: Columbia A 1011 LP: Columbia ML 2192

JERRY HERMAN (Born 1932)

Bosom buddies

New York 1967	Thebom	LP: Legendary LR 200

ROBERT KATSCHER (Born 1894)

When day is done

New York 9 December 1949	Firestone Orchestra Barlow	78: Columbia MM 906 45: Columbia A 906 LP: Columbia ML 2105
Date not confirmed	Vann, piano	LP: Private issue SLS 7413

JEROME KERN (1885-1945)

All the things you are

New York 3 January 1946	Firestone Orchestra	LP: Legendary LR 141 CD: Box Office ENBO 4
New York 13 February 1950	Firestone Orchestra	VHS Video: Bel Canto Society 69134

The touch of your hand

New York 7 September 1947	Victor Orchestra Blackton	78: Victor 10-1248 LP: Ariel OMB 15

RICHARD KOUNTZ

The sleigh

New York 25 December 1950	Firestone Orchestra Barlow	VHS Video: Bel Canto Society 69113
New York December 1977	Biltcliffe, piano	LP: Steber Music Foundation ESMF 4-5

Santa Claus is coming to town

New York 20 December 1954	Firestone Orchestra Pelletier	VHS Video: Bel Canto Society 69113

FRITZ KREISLER (1875-1962)

Stars in my eyes

New York 7 September 1947	Victor Orchestra Blackton	78: Victor 10-1248
New York 4 October 1973	Biltcliffe, piano Rabb, violin	LP: RCA ARL1-0436

ERNST KRENEK (1900-1991)

Ballad of the railroads

New York 5 April 1950	Mitropoulos, piano	Unpublished radio broadcast

JOHN LAMONTAINE

Songs of the rose of Sharon

Trenton NJ 13 January 1962	Trenton SO Harsanyi	LP: Private issue SLS 7420

Stopping by woods on a snowy evening

Date not confirmed	Biltcliffe, piano	LP: Private issue SLP 411-412/ SLPS 7411-7412 LP: Desto D 411-412

FRANZ LEHAR (1870-1948)

Die lustige Witwe, excerpts (Viljalied; Lippen schweigen)

New York 7 September 1947	Victor Orchestra Blackton	78: Victor 11-9218
New York 2 January 1950	Firestone Orchestra	VHS Video: Bel Canto Society 69122
New York 4 October 1973	Biltcliffe, piano Rabb, violin	LP: RCA ARL1-0436

RUGGIERO LEONCAVALLO (1858-1919)

I pagliacci, excerpt (Stridono lassù)

New York 2 January 1950	Firestone Orchestra	VHS Video: Bel Canto Society 69122

I pagliacci, excerpt (A quest' ora che imprudenza)

Philadelphia 17 June 1940	Warren, Cehanovsky Philadelphia Orchestra Pelletier	78: World's Greatest Music SR 70-72 LP: Victor CAL 226/CFL 101 CD: VAI Audio VAIA 10722 78 edition published without artists' names

SAMUEL LIDDLE (1867-1951)

The Lord is my shepherd; How lovely are thy dwellings

Date not confirmed	Biltcliffe, organ	LP: Private issue SLP 404

FRANK LOESSER (1910-1969)

Lovelier than ever

New York 28 May 1951	Firestone Orchestra	VHS Video: Bel Canto Society 69112

MACLELLAN

Beautiful lady

New York 2 January 1950	Firestone Orchestra	VHS Video: Bel Canto Society 69134

ALBERT MALOTTE (1895-1964)

The Lord's prayer

Date not confirmed	Biltcliffe, organ	LP: Private issue SLP 404

JULES MASSENET (1842-1912)

Hérodiade, excerpt (Il est doux, il est bon)

New York 14 February 1949	Firestone Orchestra Barlow	CD: VAI Audio VAIA 10722

Manon, excerpt (Je marche sur tous les chemins)

New York 2 November 1953	Firestone Orchestra	VHS Video: Bel Canto Society 69122
New York 4 October 1973	Biltcliffe, piano	LP: RCA ARL1-0436

FELIX MENDELSSOHN-BARTHOLDY (1809-1847)

Elijah, excerpt (Hear ye Israel!)

New York 8 June 1942	Victor Orchestra O'Connell	Victor unpublished
New York 18 September 1951	Columbia SO Rudolf	LP: Columbia ML 4521/ML 5226/P 14171 CD: Sony MHK 62356

GIAN CARLO MENOTTI (Born 1911)

The Telephone, excerpt (Telephone aria)

New York 1956	Biltcliffe, piano	CD: VAI Audio VAIA 10052

JAMES MOLLOY (1839-1909)

Love's old sweet song

New York 24 December 1947	Russ Case Orchestra	78: Victor M 1243
Date not confirmed	Vann, piano	LP: Private issue SLS 7413

WILLIAM MONK (1823-1889)

Abide with me

New York 19 December 1947	Harshaw Victor Orchestra Case	78: Victor 10-1463 45: Victor 49-1026
Date not confirmed	Biltcliffe, organ	LP: Private issue SLP 404

DOUGLAS MOORE (1893-1969)

Death be not proud

Date not confirmed	Biltcliffe, piano	LP: Private issue SLP 411-412/ SLPS 7411-7412 LP: Desto D 411-412

MOYA

Song of songs

New York 17 April 1950	Firestone Orchestra	VHS Video: Bel Canto Society 69134

WOLFGANG AMADEUS MOZART (1756-1791)

A questo seno deh vieni, concert aria

New York April 1960	Symphony of the Air R.Lawrence	LP: Private issue SLP 406/SLS 7406 CD: VAI Audio VAIA 10312

Bella mia fiamma, concert aria

New York April 1960	Symphony of the Air R.Lawrence	LP: Private issue SLP 406/SLS 7406 CD: VAI Audio VAIA 10312

Così fan tutte

New York 12 January 1952	Role of Fiordiligi Munsel, Thebom, Tucker, Guarrera, Brownlee Metropolitan Opera Orchestra & Chorus Stiedry Sung in English	Unpublished Met broadcast
New York 4-6 June 1952	Peters, Thebom, Tucker, Guarrera, Alvary Metropolitan Opera Orchestra & Chorus Stiedry Sung in English	LP: Columbia SL 122/Y3-32670
New York 7 February 1953	Peters, Thebom, Tucker, Guarrera, Brownlee Metropolitan Opera Orchestra & Chorus Stiedry	Unpublished Met broadcast
New York 10 April 1954	Munsel, Thebom, Tucker, Guarrera, Brownlee Metropolitan Opera Orchestra & Chorus Stiedry	Unpublished Met broadcast
New York 17 December 1955	Munsel, Thebom, Valletti, Guarrera, Alvary Metropolitan Opera Orchestra & Chorus Stiedry	Unpublished Met broadcast

E
L
E
A
N
O
R

S
T
E
B
E
R

WIGMORE HALL

Saturday, 6th February at 7.30 p.m.

Saturday, 13th February at 7.30 p.m.

Saturday, 20th February at 7.30 p.m.

with GERALD MOORE

Programme and Notes — One Shilling

PROGRAMME

Saturday, 6th February, 1965, at 7.30 p.m.

Zeffiretti lusinghieri — *Mozart*
from " Idomeneo "

Per pietà bell' idol mio — *Mozart*
from " Cosi fan Tutte "

Hermit Songs — *Barber*
At Saint Patrick's Purgatory
Church Bell at Night
St. Ita's Vision
The Heavenly Banquet
The Crucifixion
Sea-Snatch
Promiscuity
The Monk and his Cat
The Praises of God
The Desire for Hermitage

INTERVAL

Blumenlieder — *Schubert*
Blumenlied (*Hölty*)
Blumenbrief (*Schreiber*)
Viola (Blumenballade by *Schober*)
Der Blumenschmerz (*Maylath*)
Die Blumensprache (*Platner*)

" Lucrezia " — *Händel*
Cantata for Solo Soprano

PROGRAMME

Saturday, 13th February, 1965, at 7.30 p.m.

Die Ehre Gottes aus der Natur — *Beethoven*

Ich liebe dich

Wonne der Wehmuth

An die ferne Geliebte

Pause

Sieben frühe Lieder — *Alban Berg*

Nacht (*Hauptmann*)
Schilflied (*Lenau*)
Nachtigall (*Storm*)
Traumgekrönt (*Rilke*)
In dem Zimmer (*Schlaf*)
Liebesode (*Hartleben*)
Sommertage (*Hohenberg*)

Lebenslieder — *R. Strauss*

Ich liebe Dich
Freundliche Vision
Hochzeitlich Lied
Meinem Kinde
Du meines Herzens Krönelein
Befreit
Morgen

PROGRAMME

Saturday, 20th February, 1965, at 7.30 p.m.

Geistliche Lieder *Wolf*
from " Spanisches Liederbuch "

Nun bin ich dein

Die du Gott gebarst, du Reine

Nun wandre Maria

Die ihr schwebet

Führ mich, Kind, nach Bethlehem

Ach, des Knaben Augen

Mühvoll komm ich und beladen

Ach, wie lang die Seele schlummert

Herr, was trägt der Boden hier

Wunden trägst du, mein Geliebter

INTERVAL

Cinq Poèmes de Baudelaire *Debussy*

Le Balcon

Harmonie du Soir

Le jet d'eau

Recueillement

La mort des amants

Winter Words *Britten*

At Day-close in November

Wagtail and Baby (A Satire)

The Choirmaster's Burial
(Or the Tenor Man's story)

Proud Songsters
(Thrushes, Finches and Nightingales)

At the Railway Station, Upway
(or the Convict and Boy with the Violin)

Before Life and After

Così fan tutte, excerpt (Come scoglio)

New York 4 October 1973	Biltcliffe, piano	LP: RCA ARL1-0436

Così fan tutte, excerpt (Per pietà)

New York 14-21 February 1953	Columbia SO Walter	LP: Columbia ML 4694/3216 0363 CD: Sony SM3K 47211

Don Giovanni

New York 9 December 1944	<u>Role of Elvira</u> Kirk, Sayao, Kullmann, Pinza, Baccaloni, Harrell, Moscona Metropolitan Opera Orchestra & Chorus Szell	Unpublished Met broadcast
New York 13 March 1954	Harshaw, Conner, Conley, London, Corena, Vickery, Alvary Metropolitan Opera Orchestra & Chorus Rudolf	Unpublished Met broadcast
New York 14 February 1959	<u>Role of Anna</u> Della Casa, Hurley, Valletti, London, Flagello, Wildermann, Uppman Metropolitan Opera Orchestra & Chorus Böhm	LP: Melodram MEL 439
New York 14 January 1961	Della Casa, Hurley, Gedda, Siepi, Corena, Wildermann, Uppman Metropolitan Opera Orchestra & Chorus Leinsdorf	Unpublished Met broadcast

Don Giovanni, excerpt (Mi tradi)

New York 5 September 1947	Victor Orchestra Blackton	78: Victor 11-9114
New York 14-21 February 1953	Columbia SO Walter	LP: Columbia ML 4694/3216 0363 CD: Sony SM3K 47211
Graz 4 August 1979	Evans, piano	LP: Steber Music Foundation ESMF 6-7

Don Giovanni, excerpt (Or sai chi l'onore)

New York 1957		CD: Legato BIM 712

Don Giovanni, excerpt (Non mi dir)

New York 14-21 February 1953	Columbia SO Walter	LP: Columbia ML 4694/3216 0363 CD: Sony SM3K 47211

Die Entführung aus dem Serail

New York 18 January 1947	Role of Konstanze Alarie, Kullmann, Garris, Ernster Metropolitan Opera Orchestra & Chorus Cooper Sung in English	Unpublished Met broadcast

Die Entführung aus dem Serail, excerpt (Martern aller Arten)

New York 13 March 1947	Victor Orchestra Morel Sung in English	78: Victor DM 1157/11-9773 45: Victor WDM 1157 LP: Victor VIC 1455 CD: RCA/BMG GD 60521
New York 10 October 1958	Biltcliffe, piano	LP: Private issue SLP 101 CD: VAI Audio VAIA 10052

Die Entführung aus dem Serail, excerpt (Traurigkeit ward mir zum Lose)

New York 14-21 February 1953	Columbia SO Walter	LP: Columbia ML 4694/3216 0363 CD: Sony SM3K 47211

Die Entführung aus dem Serail, excerpt (Ach ich liebte)

New York 13 March 1947	Victor Orchestra Morel Sung in English	Victor unpublished

Exsultate jubilate

Philadelphia 15 November 1953	Philadelphia Orchestra Ormandy	Columbia unpublished
New York April 1960	Symphony of the Air R.Lawrence	LP: Private issue SLP 406/SLS 7406 CD: VAI Audio VAIA 10312

Alleluia (Exsultate jubilate)

New York 23 December 1957	Firestone Orchestra Barlow	VHS Video: Bel Canto Society 69113
New York 10 October 1958	Biltcliffe, piano	LP: Private issue SLP 101 CD: Legato BIM 712 CD: VAI Audio VAIA 10052
Graz 4 August 1979	Evans, piano	LP: Steber Music Foundation ESMF 6-7

Idomeneo, excerpt (Zeffiretti lusinghieri)

New York 10 October 1958	Biltcliffe, piano	LP: Private issue SLP 101 CD: VAI Audio VAIA 10052
New York 4 October 1973	Biltcliffe, piano	LP: RCA ARL1-0436

Idomeneo, excerpt (D'Oreste d'Ajace!)

New York April 1960	Symphony of the Air R.Lawrence	LP: Private issue SLP 406/SLS 7406 CD: VAI Audio VAIA 10312

Nehmt meinen Dank, concert aria

New York April 1960	Symphony of the Air R.Lawrence	LP: Private issue SLP 406/SLS 7406 CD: VAI Audio VAIA 10312
Graz 4 August 1979	Evans, piano	LP: Steber Music Foundation ESMF 6-7

Le nozze di Figaro

New York 17 April 1943	Role of Contessa Sayao, Novotna, Pinza, Brownlee Metropolitan Opera Orchestra & Chorus Breisach	Unpublished Met broadcast
New York 29 January 1944	Sayao, Novotna, Pinza, Brownlee Metropolitan Opera Orchestra & Chorus Walter	LP: Discocorp MLG 75-77 LP: Operatic Archives POA 1033-1035 Excerpts CD: Legato BIM 712
New York 15 March 1947	Schymberg, Novotna, Pinza, Brownlee Metropolitan Opera Orchestra & Chorus Busch	Unpublished Met broadcast
New York 8 January 1949	Sayao, Novotna, Tajo, Brownlee Metropolitan Opera Orchestra & Chorus Busch	Unpublished Met broadcast
New York 11 February 1950	Sayao, Novotna, Tajo, Brownlee Metropolitan Opera Orchestra & Chorus Reiner	Unpublished Met broadcast
New York 15 January 1955	Conner, Miller, Tajo, Guarrera Metropolitan Opera Orchestra & Chorus Stiedry	Unpublished Met broadcast

Le nozze di Figaro, excerpt (Porgi amor)

New York 22 February 1945	Victor Orchestra Leinsdorf	78: Victor DM 1157/11-8850 45: Victor WDM 1157/49-0646 CD: RCA/BMG GD 60521
London 17 September 1947	Philharmonia Susskind	HMV unpublished
New York 18 February 1952	Firestone Orchestra Barlow	CD: VAI Audio VAIA 10312 VHS Video: Bel Canto society 69102
Graz 4 August 1979	Evans, piano	LP: Steber Music Foundation ESMF 6-7

Le nozze di Figaro, excerpt (Dove sono)

New York 22 February 1945	Victor Orchestra Leinsdorf	78: Victor DM 1157/11-8850 45: Victor WDM 1157/49-0646 CD: RCA/BMG GD 60521
London 17 September 1947	Philharmonia Susskind	HMV unpublished
New York 17 September 1951	Firestone Orchestra Barlow	CD: VAI Audio VAIA 10312 VHS Video: Bel Canto Society 69102
New York 14-21 February 1953	Columbia SO Walter	LP: Columbia ML 4694/3216 0363 LP: CBS 30053 CD: Sony MDK 46579/SM3K 47211 CD: Metropolitan Opera MET 211
Graz 4 August 1979	Evans, piano	LP: Steber Music Foundation ESMF 6-7

Le nozze di Figaro, excerpt (Deh vieni non tardar)

New York 19 February 1947	Victor Orchestra Morel	78: Victor DM 1157/11-9772 45: Victor WDM 1157 CD: RCA/BMG GD 60521
New York 4 September 1950	Firestone Orchestra Pelletier	CD: VAI Audio VAIA 10312 VHS Video: Bel Canto Society 69122

Le nozze di Figaro, excerpt (Voi che sapete)

New York 16 September 1946	Firestone Orchestra Barlow	CD: VAI Audio VAIA 10312
New York 19 February 1947	Victor Orchestra Morel	78: Victor 12-0526

Le nozze di Figaro, excerpt (Non so più)

New York 19 February 1947	Victor Orchestra Morel	78: Victor DM 1157/11-9772 45: Victor WDM 1157 CD: RCA/BMG GD 60521

Il re pastore, excerpt (L'amero sarò costante)

New York April 1960	Symphony of the Air R.Lawrence	LP: Private issue SLP 406/SLS 7406 CD: VAI Audio VAIA 10312

Der Schauspieldirektor, excerpt (Bester Jüngling!)

New York 14-21 February 1953	Columbia SO Walter	LP: Columbia ML 4694/3216 0363 CD: Sony SM3K 47211

Die Zauberflöte

New York 10 January 1942	Role of 1st Lady Novotna, Bok, Bodanya, Kullmann, Kipnis, Brownlee, Schorr Metropolitan Opera Orchestra & Chorus Walter Sung in English	CD: Walhall WHL 2
New York 26 December 1942	Conner, Antoine, Raymondi, Kullmann, Pinza, Brownlee, Cordon Metropolitan Opera Orchestra & Chorus Walter	Unpublished Met broadcast
New York 1 April 1944	Conner, Bowman, Raymondi, Kullmann, Kipnis, Brownlee, Moscona Metropolitan Opera Orchestra & Chorus Walter	Unpublished Met broadcast
New York 25 November 1950	Role of Pamina Berger, Raymondi, Tucker, Hines, Brownlee, Schöffler Metropolitan Opetra Orchestra & Chorus Stiedry	Unpublished Met broadcast

Die Zauberflöte, excerpt (Ach ich fühl's)

New York 5 September 1945	Victor Orchestra Leinsdorf Sung in English	78: Victor 11-9114 CD: RCA/BMG GD 60521 CD: Metropolitan Opera MET 517
New York 14-21 February 1953	Columbia SO Walter	LP: Columbia ML 4694/3216 0363 CD: Sony SM3K 47211
New York 4 October 1973	Biltcliffe, piano	LP: RCA ARL1-0436

Lieder: An Chloe; Abendempfindung; Das Veilchen; Das Lied der Trennung; Der Liebe himmlisches Gefühl; Die ihr des unermesslichen Weltalls; Die Zufriedenheit; Komm lieber Zither!

Graz 4 August 1979	Evans, piano	LP: Steber Music Foundation ESMF 6-7

HORATIO PARKER (1863-1919)

Oh country bright and fair!/Hora novissima

New York 8 June 1942	Victor Orchestra O'Connell	Victor unpublished

ARTHUR PENN (1875-1941)

Smilin' through

New York 10 December 1947	Russ Case Orchestra	78: Victor M 1243
Date not confirmed	Vann, piano	LP: Private issue SLS 7413

COLE PORTER (1891-1964)

Every time we say goodbye

New York 9 December 1949	Firestone Orchestra Barlow	78: Columbia MM 906 45: Columbia A 906 LP: Columbia ML 2105
New York 15 May 1950	Firestone Orchestra	VHS Video: Bel Canto Society 69134

I love you

Date not confirmed	Vann, piano	LP: Private issue SLS 7413

So in love

New York 26 June 1950	Firestone Orchestra	VHS Video: Bel Canto Society 69134
New York 9 June 1952	Firestone Orchestra Barlow	VHS Video: Bel Canto Society 69102

GIACOMO PUCCINI (1858-1924)

La Bohème, excerpt (Si mi chiamano Mimì)

New York 7 March 1949	Firestone Orchestra Sung in English	CD: VAI Audio VAIA 10722
New York 27 November 1950	Firestone Orchestra	VHS Video: Bel Canto Society 69122

La Bohème, excerpt (O soave fanciulla)

New York 25-26 June 1940	Tokatayan Metropolitan Opera Orchestra Pelletier	78: World's Greatest Music SR 61-62 LP: Victor CAL 222/CFL 101 CD: VAI Audio VAIA 10232 78 edition published without artists' names

La Bohème, excerpt (Addio dolce svegliare)

New York 25-26 June 1940	Dickey, Tokatayan, Cehanovsky, Alvary Metropolitan Opera Orchestra Pelletier	78: World's Greatest Music SR 61-62 LP: Victor CAL 222/CFL 101 CD: VAI Audio VAIA 10232 78 edition published without artists' names

La Bohème, excerpt (Sono andati...to end of opera)

New York 25-26 June 1940	Dickey, Tokatatan, Cehanovsky, Alvary Metropolitan Opera Orchestra Pelletier	78: World's Greatest Music SR 61-62 LP: Victor CAL 222/CFL 101 CD: VAI Audio VAIA 10232 78 edition published without artists' names

La Bohème, excerpt (Quando m'en vo)

New York 20 March 1950	Firestone Orchestra Sung in English	VHS Video: Bel Canto Society 69122
New York 1958		CD: Legato BIM 712
New York 4 October 1973	Biltcliffe, piano	LP: RCA ARL1-0436

La fanciulla del West

Florence 15 June 1954	Role of Minnie Del Monaco, Guelfi Maggio musicale Orchestra & Chorus Mitropoulos	LP: Cetra LO 64/DOC 41 CD: Hunt CD 565 Excerpts CD: Legato BIM 712

Gianni Schicchi, excerpt (O mio babbino caro)

New York 11 July 1949	Firestone Orchestra	CD: VAI Audio VAIA 10722

Madama Butterfly

Los Angeles 3 September 1948	Role of Butterfly Carré, Peerce, Bonelli Hollywood Bowl SO and Chorus Ormandy	CD: Eklipse EKRCD 16
New York 26-28 May 1949	Madeira, Tucker, Valdengo Metropolitan Opera Orchestra & Chorus Rudolf	LP: Columbia SL 104/Y3-32107 LP: CBS 78246 Excerpts LP: CBS 30067

Madama Butterfly, excerpt (Un bel dì)

New York 26 June 1940	Metropolitan Opera Orchestra Pelletier	78: World's Greatest Music SR 58-60 LP: Victor CAL 222/CFL 101 LP: Legendary LR 141 CD: VAI Audio VAIA 10232 CD: Legato BIM 712 78 edition published without artists' names
New York 2 August 1954	Firestone Orchestra	VHS Video: Bel Canto Society 69112
New York 10 October 1958	Biltcliffe, piano	LP: Private issue SLP 101 CD: RCA/BMG GD 60521 CD: VAI Audio VAIA 10052

Madama Butterfly, excerpt (Bimba dagli occhi/Viene la sera)

New York 26 June 1940	Tokatayan Metropolitan Opera Orchestra Pelletier	78: World's Greatest Music SR 58-60 LP: Victor CAL 222/CFL 101 CD: VAI Audio VAIA 10232 78 edition published without artists' names

Madama Butterfly, excerpt (Ancora un passo)

New York 30 May 1940	Metropolitan Opera Orchestra & Chorus Pelletier	78: World's Greatest Music SR 58-60 LP: Victor CAL 222/CFL 101 CD: VAI Audio VAIA 10232 78 edition published without artists' names

Madama Butterfly, excerpt (Scuoti quella fronda)

New York 26 June 1940	Browning Metropolitan Opera Orchestra Pelletier	78: World's Greatest Music SR 58-60 LP: Victor CAL 222/CFL 101 CD: VAI Audio VAIA 10232 78 edition published without artists' names

Madama Butterfly, excerpt (Con onor muore)

New York 31 May 1940	Metropolitan Opera Orchestra Pelletier	78: World's Greatest Music SR 58-60 LP: Victor CAL 222/CFL 101 CD: VAI Audio VAIA 10232 78 edition published without artists' names

Tosca

New York 11 April 1959	Role of Tosca Bergonzi, London Metropolitan Opera Orchestra & Chorus Adler	CD: Myto MCD 951.120

Tosca, excerpt (Vissi d'arte)

New York 5 December 1949	Firestone Orchestra Barlow	VHS Video: Bel Canto Society 69110
New York 17 April 1950	Firestone Orchestra	VHS Video: Bel Canto Society 69122
New York 10 October 1958	Biltcliffe, piano	CD: VAI Audio VAIA 10052
New York 4 October 1973	Biltcliffe, piano	LP: RCA ARL1-0436
Boston 20 April 1975	Rogers, piano	LP: Steber Music Foundation ESMF 1

Turandot, excerpt (Signore ascolta)

New York 10 March 1946	Firestone Orchestra Sung in English	LP: Legendary LR 141 CD: Legato BIM 712 CD: VAI Audio VAIA 10722

JEAN PHILIPPE RAMEAU (1683-1764)

Le berger fidèle

Syracuse NY 1962	I.Kipnis ensemble I.Kipnis	LP: Private issue SLS 7416

OSCAR RASBACH (1888-1975)

Trees

Date not confirmed	Vann, piano	LP: Private issue SLS 7413

RICHARD RODGERS (1902-1979)

Oklahoma, highlights

New York 13-22 December 1944	Melton, Thomas Victor Orchestra	78: Victor M 988 People will say we're in love LP: Victor DPL 90100

If I loved you

New York 7 September 1946	Firestone Orchestra	LP: Legendary LR 141 LP: Startone ST 223

It's a grand night for singing

New York 27 November 1950	Firestone Orchestra	VHS Video: Bel Canto Society 69134

Out of my dreams

New York 14 November 1949	Firestone Orchestra Barlow	LP: Legendary LR 142 VHS Video: Bel Canto Society 69102
New York 9 December 1949	Firestone Orchestra Barlow	78: Columbia MM 906 45: Columbia A 906 LP: Columbia ML 2105

SIGMUND ROMBERG (1887-1951)

New Moon, selection

New York 7 September 1950	Eddy Orchestra and Chorus Arnaud	78: Columbia MM 975 45: Columbia A 975 LP: Columbia ML 2164/P 13878 One kiss LP: Columbia P6-1503

When I grow too old to dream

New York 9 December 1949	Firestone Orchestra Barlow	78: Columbia MM 906 45: Columbia A 906 LP: Columbia ML 2105
Date not confirmed	Vann, piano	LP: Private issue SLS 7413

Will you remember?

New York 21 January 1946	Björling Firestone Orchestra Barlow	LP: Ed Smith EJS 367 LP: Legendary LR 141 CD: Legato BIM 712
New York 5 December 1949	Warren Firestone Orchestra Barlow	VHS Video: Bel Canto Society 69110

NED ROREM (Born 1923)

Alleluja

Date not confirmed	Biltcliffe, piano	LP: Private issue SLP 411-412/ SLPS 7411-7412 LP: Desto D 411-412

GIOACHINO ROSSINI (1792-1868)

Il barbiere di Siviglia, excerpt (Una voce poco fa)

New York 1 February 1944		CD: VAI Audio VAIA 10722
New York 16 May 1946		LP: Legendary LR 141 CD: Legato BIM 712

Stabat mater, excerpt (Inflammatus)

New York 19 March 1951	Firestone Orchestra	CD: VAI Audio VAIA 10722 VHS Video: Bel Canto Society 69122

ALESSANDRO SCARLATTI (1660-1725)

Christmas cantata

New York December 1977	Stony Baroque Players	LP: Steber Music Foundation ESMF 4-5

FRANZ SCHUBERT (1797-1828)

Auflösung

New York 1-5 May 1941	Quillan, piano	78: Victor 10-1099

Im Abendrot

New York 1956	Biltcliffe, piano	CD: VAI Audio VAIA 10052

Ständchen

New York 1956	Biltcliffe, piano	CD: VAI Audio VAIA 10052

ARTHUR SCHWARTZ (1900-1984)

Dancing in the dark

New York 31 July 1950	Firestone Orchestra	VHS Video: Bel Canto Society 69134

You and the night and the music

New York 9 December 1949	Firestone Orchestra Barlow	78: Columbia MM 906 45: Columbia A 906 LP: Columbia ML 2105
New York 27 October 1952	Firestone Orchestra	VHS Video: Bel Canto Society 69134

ERNEST SEITZ (1892-1978)

The world is waiting for the sunrise

New York 2 August 1954	Firestone Orchestra	VHS Video: Bel Canto Society 69112
Date not confirmed	Vann, piano	LP: Private issue SLS 7413

RUDOLF SIECZYNSKI (1879-1952)

Wien du Stadt meiner Träume

New York 4 October 1973	Biltcliffe, piano Rabb, violin	LP: RCA ARL1-0436

OLEY SPEAKS (1874-1948)

Morning

New York 14 November 1949	Firestone Orchestra Barlow	VHS Video: Bel Canto Society 69102

OSCAR STRAUS (1870-1954)

Der tapfere Soldat, excerpt (Komm Held meiner Träume!)

New York 5 December 1949	Firestone Orchestra Barlow Sung in English	VHS Video: Bel Canto Society 69110
New York 15 May 1950	Firestone Orchestra Sung in English	VHS Video: Bel Canto Society 69134
New York 28 May 1951	Firestone Orchestra Sung in English	VHS Video: Bel Canto Society 69112

JOHANN STRAUSS (1825-1899)

Die Fledermaus, excerpt (Klänge der Heimat)

New York 30 November 1953	Firestone Orchestra Sung in English	LP: Legendary LR 141 CD: Legato BIM 712 VHS Video: Bel Canto Society 69112

RICHARD STRAUSS (1864-1949)

Arabella

New York 26 February 1955	Role of Arabella Güden, Peters, Thebom, Votipka, Sullivan, London, Herbert Metropolitan Opera Orchestra & Chorus Kempe Sung in English	CD: Voce della luna VL 2014 US premiere performances of the opera

Die Frau ohne Schatten, excerpt (Ist mein Liebster dahin?)

New York 10 October 1958	Biltcliffe, piano	LP: Private issue SLP 101 CD: VAI Audio VAIA 10052

Die Frau ohne Schatten, excerpt (Sieh Amme!/Würde ich lieber selber zu Stein!)

Munich 4 June 1953	Steingruber Bavarian RO Böhm	CD: VAI Audio VAIA 10122

Die Frau ohne Schatten, excerpt (Vater bist du's?)

Munich 4 June 1953	Steingruber, Goltz, Svanholm, Wiener Bavarian RO Böhm	CD: VAI Audio VAIA 10122 This recording continues to end of opera
New York 10 October 1958	Biltcliffe, piano	LP: Private issue SLP 101 CD: VAI Audio VAIA 10052 This recording concludes after Zeige dich Vater!

Freundliche Vision

New York 1956	Biltcliffe, piano	CD: VAI Audio VAIA 10052

Der Rosenkavalier

New York 14 December 1946	<u>Role of Sophie</u> Jessner, Stevens, Baum, List, Lechner Metropolitan Opera Orchestra & Chorus Busch	Unpublished Met broadcast
New York 14 February 1948	Jessner, Novotna, Baum, List, Lechner Metropolitan Opera Orchestra & Chorus Busch	Unpublished Met broadcast
New York 21 November 1949	<u>Role of Marschallin</u> Berger, Stevens, Di Stefano, List, Thompson Metropolitan Opera Orchestra & Chorus Reiner	Unpublished video recording
New York 3 December 1949	Berger, Stevens, Di Stefano, List, Thompson Metropolitan Opera Orchestra & Chorus Reiner	CD: Arlecchino ARLA 37-39 <u>Excerpt</u> CD: International Record Collector IRCC 809

4 letzte Lieder

Cleveland 5 May 1970	Cleveland Orchestra Levine	CD: VAI Audio VAIA 10122

ALEC TEMPLETON (1909-1963)

Roses in wintertime; Vienna in springtime

New York 24 December 1947	Templeton, piano	78: Victor 10-1473 45: Victor 49-0421

AMBROISE THOMAS (1811-1896)

Mignon, excerpt (Je suis Titania!)

New York 8 February 1942	Orchestra Goossens	CD: VAI Audio VAIA 10722

VIRGIL THOMSON (1896-1989)

The tiger

Date not confirmed	Biltcliffe, piano	LP: Private issue SLP 411-412/ SLPS 7411-7412 LP: Desto D 411-412

GIUSEPPE VERDI (1813-1901)

Don Carlo

New York 5 March 1955	Role of Elisabetta Thebom, Tucker, Bastianini, Hines, Moscona Metropolitan Opera Orchestra & Chorus Adler	LP: Estro armonico EA 043 CD: Myto MCD 946.116

Don Carlo, excerpt (Tu che la vanità)

New York 16 August 1950	Metropolitan Opera Orchestra Cleva	78: Columbia MX 351 LP: Columbia ML 2157/Y 31149 LP: Philips NBR 6037/N02609R

Ernani, excerpt (Ernani involami!)

New York 10 March 1940	Orchestra	CD: VAI Audio VAIA 10722
New York 17 August 1950	Metropolitan Opera Orchestra Cleva	78: Columbia MX 351 LP: Columbia ML 2157/Y 31149 LP: Philips NBR 6037/N02609R
New York 28 May 1951	Firestone Orchestra	VHS Video: Bel Canto Society 69112
New York 10 October 1958	Biltcliffe, piano	LP: Private issue SLP 101 CD: RCA/BMG GD 60521 CD: VAI Audio VAIA 10052

La forza del destino, excerpt (Pace pace mio Dio!)

New York 17 August 1950	Metropolitan Opera Orchestra Cleva	78: Columbia MX 351 LP: Columbia ML 2157/Y 31149 LP: Philips NBR 6037/N02609R
New York 9 June 1952	Firestone Orchestra Barlow	VHS Video: Bel Canto Society 69102
New York 7 December 1974	Biltcliffe, piano	LP: Steber Music Foundation ESMF 1

Otello

New York 9 February 1952	<u>Role of Desdemona</u> Lipton, Vinay, Hayward, Warren Metropolitan Opera Orchestra & Chorus Stiedry	Unpublished Met broadcast

Otello, excerpt (Già nella notte)

New York 31 December 1951	Vinay Metropolitan Opera Orchestra Cleva	LP: Columbia ML 4499/Y 31149 LP: Philips ABL 3005/N02102L

Otello, excerpt (Dio ti giocondi)

New York 31 December 1951	Vinay Metropolitan Opera Orchestra Cleva	LP: Columbia ML 4499/Y 31149 LP: Philips ABL 3005/N02102L CD: Metropolitan Opera MET 514

Otello, excerpt (Piangea cantando)

New York 16 August 1950	Metropolitan Opera Orchestra Cleva	78: Columbia MX 351 LP: Columbia ML 2157/ML 4499/Y 31149 LP: Philips ABL 3005/NBR 6037/ N02102L/N02609R
New York 1958		CD: Legato BIM 712

Otello, excerpt (Ave Maria)

New York 16 August 1950	Metropolitan Opera Orchestra Cleva	78: Columbia MX 351 LP: Columbia ML 2157/ML 4499/Y 31149 LP: Philips ABL 3005/NBR 6037/ N02102L/N02609R
New York 19 March 1951	Firestone Orchestra	VHS Video: Bel Canto Society 69112
New York 1958		CD: Legato BIM 712

Rigoletto, excerpt (Bella figlia dell' amore)

New York 30 November 1953	Stevens, Sullivan, Thomas Firestone Orchestra	LP: Legendary LR 141 VHS Video: Bel Canto Society 69112

Il trovatore, excerpt (Quel son! Quelle preci!)

New York 21 January 1946	Björling Firestone Orchestra Barlow	LP: Ed Smith EJS 367 LP: Legendary LR 141 CD: Legato BIM 712

La traviata

New York 22 January 1949	Role of Violetta Di Stefano, Merrill Metropolitan Opera Orchestra & Chorus Antonicelli	LP: Melodram MEL 308

La traviata, excerpt (Libiamo ne' lieti calici)

New York 31 May 1940	Tokayatan Metropolitan Opera Orchestra & Chorus Pelletier	78: World's Greatest Music SR 67-69 LP: Victor CAL 227/CFL 101 CD: VAI Audio VAIA 10722 78 edition published without artists' names

La traviata, excerpt (Ah fors' è lui!/Sempre libera!)

New York 25 June 1940	Metropolitan Opera Orchestra Pelletier	78: World'd Greatest Music SR 67-69 LP: Victor CAL 227/CFL 101 CD: VAI Audio VAIA 10722 CD: RCA/BMG GD 60521 CD: Metropolitan Opera MET 505 78 edition published without artists' names
New York 26 June 1941	Victor Orchestra O'Connell	Victor unpublished
New York 13 February 1950	Firestone Orchestra	VHS Video: Bel Canto Society 69122
New York 17 August 1950	Metropolitan Opera Orchestra Cleva	78: Columbia MX 351 LP: Columbia ML 2157/Y 31149 LP: Philips NBR 6037/N02609R

La traviata, excerpt (Addio del passato)

New York 1948		CD: Legato BIM 712
New York 1 May 1950	Firestone Orchestra	VHS Video: Bel Canto Society 69122

La traviata, excerpt (Parigi o cara)

New York 25 June 1940	Tokayatan Metropolitan Opera Orchestra Pelletier	78: World's Greatest Music SR 67-69 LP: Victor CAL 227/CFL 101 CD: VAI Audio VAIA 10722 78 edition published without artists' names
New York 3 January 1946	Melton Firestone Orchestra	LP: Legendary LR 141

RICHARD WAGNER (1813-1883)

Lohengrin

New York 11 April 1953	Role of Elsa Harshaw, Sullivan, S.Björling, Ernster, Budney Metropolitan Opera Orchestra & Chorus Stiedry	Unpublished Met broadcast
Bayreuth August 1953	Varnay, Windgassen, Uhde, Greindl, Braun Bayreuth Festival Orchestra & Chorus Keilberth	LP: Decca LXT 2880-2884/D12 D5 LP: London A 4502/RS 65003 CD: Teldec 4509 936742
New York 24 December 1955	Harshaw, Sullivan, Edelmann, Uhde, Budney Metropolitan Opera Orchestra & Chorus Stiedry	Unpublished Met broadcast

Lohengrin, excerpt (Einsam in trüben Tagen)

New York 25 May 1953	Firestone Orchestra	VHS Video: Bel Canto Society 69122

Die Meistersinger von Nürnberg

New York 15 December 1945	Role of Eva Thorborg, Kullmann, Garris, Gynrod, List, Pechner Metropolitan Opera Orchestra & Chorus Szell	Unpublished Met broadcast

Tannhäuser, excerpt (Dich teure Halle)

New York 1958		CD: Legato BIM 712

CARL MARIA VON WEBER (1786-1826)

Der Freischütz, excerpt (Leise leise)

Boston 20 April 1975	Rogers, piano	LP: Steber Music Foundation ESMF 1

KURT WEILL (1900-1950)

September song

New York 17 September 1951	Firestone Orchestra Barlow	VHS Video: Bel Canto Society 69102

HUGO WOLF (1860-1903)

Elfenlied

New York 1956	Biltcliffe, piano	CD: VAI Audio VAIA 10052

Spanisches Liederbuch: Nun bin ich dein; Die du Gott gebarst; Nun wandre Maria; Die ihr schwebt um diese Palmen; Führ' mich Kind; Ach des Knaben Augen; Mühvoll komm' ich und beladen; Ach wie lang die Seele schlummert; Herr was trägt der Boden hier?; Wunden trägst du

New York 7 December 1974	Biltcliffe, piano	LP: Steber Music Foundation ESMF 1

TRADITIONAL, MISCELLEANEOUS AND CHRISTMAS CAROLS

Danny Boy, arranged by Weatherly

New York 29 July 1946	Firestone Orchestra	CD: VAI Audio VAIA 10722
New York 10 December 1947	Russ Case Orchestra	78: Victor M 1243
New York 1956	Biltcliffe, piano	CD: VAI Audio VAIA 10052
New York 1962	Vann, piano	45: Private issue SLP 45-413 LP: Private issue SLP 413/SLS 7413

Deck the halls

New York 20 December 1954	Firestone Orchestra Pelletier	VHS Video: Bel Canto Society 69113

The first Nowell

New York 20 December 1954	Firestone Orchestra Pelletier	VHS Video: Bel Canto Society 69113
New York December 1977		LP: Steber Music Foundation ESMF 4-5 With audience participation

The friendly beasts

New York 25 December 1950	Firestone Orchestra Barlow	VHS Video: Bel Canto Society 69113
New York December 1977	Stony Baroque Players	LP: Steber Music Foundation ESMF 4-5

Hark the herald angels

New York 23 December 1957	Firestone Orchestra Barlow	VHS Video: Bel Canto Society 69113

It came upon the midnight clear

New York 23 December 1957	Firestone Orchestra Barlow	VHS Video: Bel Canto Society 69113

Joy to the world

New York December 1977		LP: Steber Music Foundation ESMF 4-5 With audience participation

Nancy Hanks

New York 1956	Biltcliffe, piano	CD: VAI Audio VAIA 10052

O come all ye faithful

New York December 1977		LP: Steber Music Foundation ESMF 4-5 With audience participation

There is a green hill far away

Date not confirmed	Biltcliffe, organ	LP: Private issue SLP 404

We wish you a Happy Christmas

New York 20 December 1954	Firestone Orchestra Pelletier	VHS Video: Bel Canto Society 69113

Whistle and I'll come to you

New York 1956	Biltcliffe, piano	CD: VAI Audio VAIA 10052

Zinka Milanov
1906-1989

with additional assistance from Michael Gray

Discography compiled by John Hunt

LUDWIG VAN BEETHOVEN (1770-1827)

Missa Solemnis

New York 28 December 1940	Castagna, Björling, Kipnis Westminster Choir NBC SO Toscanini	LP: Toscanini Society ATS 1023-1024 LP: Melodram MEL 006 CD: Music and Arts ATRA 259 CD: Melodram MEL 38006 CD: Palette (Japan) PAL 3004-3006 CD: As-Disc AS 307 CD: Greenline 3LC 4003 Excerpt CD: Radio Years RY 12

VINCENZO BELLINI (1801-1835)

Norma

New York 12 February 1944	<u>Role of Norma</u> Castagna, Votipka, Jagel, Lazzari Metropolitan Opera Orchestra & Chorus Sodero	LP: Ed Smith UORC 154
New York 30 December 1944	Tourel, Votipka, Jagel, Cordon Metropolitan Opera Orchestra & Chorus Sodero	LP: Ed Smith EJS 180 CD: Myto MCD 954.137 CD: Grand Tier ENGTCD 1/92 <u>Excerpts</u> CD: Legato LCD 161
New York 27 March 1954	Thebom, Leone, Penno, Siepi Metropolitan Opera Orchestra & Chorus Cleva	LP: Melodram MEL 005

Norma, excerpt (Casta diva)

New York 16 April 1945	Victor Orchestra and Chorus Weissmann	78: Victor 11-9293 78: HMV DB 6877 LP: Victor LCT 6701 LP: HMV CSLP 504 CD: RCA/BMG GD 60074
New York 19 October 1954	NBC SO Shaw Chorale Perlea	LP: Victor VIC 1395 CD: Metropolitan Opera MET 107 <u>This version includes cabaletta</u>

Norma, excerpt (Mira, o Norma!)

New York 16 April 1945	Harshaw Victor Orchestra Weissmann	78: Victor 11-8924 LP: Victor VICS 6044 CD: RCA/BMG GD 60074

BLAGOJE BERSA (1873-1934)

All Souls' Day

New York 21 October 1954	Kunc, piano	LP: Victor LM 1915

JOHANNES BRAHMS (1833-1897)

Am Sonntagmorgen

New York 15 October 1954	Kunc, piano	LP: Victor LM 1915

Wiegenlied

New York 22 October 1954	Kunc, piano	LP: Victor LM 1915

ANTONIN DVORAK (1841-1904)

Rusalka, excerpt (O silver moon)

New York 18 September 1958	Victor Orchestra Basile	LP: Victor LM2303/LSC2303/VIC1198/VICS1198 LP: Victor (Jugoslavia) LSRCA 70924 CD: RCA/BMG GD 60074

TOMMASO GIORDANI (1733-1806)

Caro mio ben

New York 15 October 1954	Kunc, piano	LP: Victor LM 1915

UMBERTO GIORDANO (1867-1948)

Andrea Chenier

New York 4 December 1954	Role of Maddalena Glaz, Elias, Del Monaco, Warren, Baccaloni Metropolitan Opera Orchestra & Chorus Cleva	LP: MRF Records MRF 15 LP: Metropolitan Opera MET 15 CD: Metropolitan Opera MET 15 CD: Nuova Era NE 2364-2365
New York 28 December 1957	Lipton, Elias, Tucker, Warren, Corena Metropolitan Opera Orchestra & Chorus Cleva	LP: ERR 110 CD: Hunt CDMP 476 Hunt incorrectly dated 1958
New York 13 April 1966	Kriese, Casei, Tucker, Sereni, Alvary Metropolitan Opera Orchestra & Chorus Molinari-Pradelli	Unpublished Met broadcast Excerpts LP: MRF Records MRF 15 Milanov's final stage performance of a complete role

Andrea Chenier, excerpt (La mamma morta)

New York 23 September 1958	Victor Orchestra Basile	LP: Victor LM 2303/LSC 2303/VIC 1198/ VICS 1198/RL 85177 LP: Victor (Jugoslavia) LSRCA 70924 CD: RCA/BMG 09026 615802 CD: Metropolitan Opera MET 107

Andrea Chenier, excerpt (Vicino a te)

New York 16 April 1966	Tucker Metropolitan Opera Orchestra Prêtre	LP: MRF Records MRF 7 Gala farewell performance in the old Metropolitan opera house

RICHARD HAGEMAN (1882-1966)

Do not go, my love

New York 21 December 1954	Kunc, piano	LP: Victor LM 1915 CD: RCA/BMG GD 60074

BOZIDAR KUNC

Longing

New York 15 October 1954	Kunc, piano	LP: Victor LM 1915 CD: RCA/BMG GD 60074

Quivering

New York 15 October 1954	Kunc, piano	LP: Victor LM 1915 CD: RCA/BMG GD 60074

The world is empty

New York 22 October 1954	Kunc, piano	LP: Victor LM 1915

PIETRO MASCAGNI (1863-1945)

Cavalleria rusticana

New York 20 March 1943	Role of Santuzza Olheim, Kaskas, Jagel, Valentino Metropolitan Opera Orchestra & Chorus Sodero	LP: Ed Smith UORC 312 CD: Walhall WHL 34
New York 2 January- 27 February 1953	Roggero, C.Smith, Björling, Merrill Victor Orchestra Shaw Chorale Cellini	45: Victor WDM 6106 LP: Victor LM 6046/VIC 6044/VICS 6044/ VL 43534 LP: HMV ALP 1126-1128 LP: HMV (France) FALP 301-303 LP: HMV (Italy) QALP 10050-10052 CD: RCA/BMG GD 86510 Excerpts 45: Victor ERB 38 45: HMV 7ER 5047/7ER 5063 45: HMV (Italy) 7ERQ 141/7ERQ 167 LP: Victor LM 1777/LM 2269/RB 16149/ VIC 1336/VICS 1336/RL 43077/AVL1-0987 LP: Victor (Jugoslavia) LSRCA 70923 LP: HMV ALP 1247 LP: HMV (Italy) QALP 10212 LP: RCA (Germany) KR 11041 CD: Metropolitan Opera MET 107 CD: RCA/BMG 09026 684292
New York 22 March 1957	Votipka, Elias, Tucker, Valentino Metropolitan Opera Orchestra & Chorus Cleva	LP: Melodram MEL 024
Boston 13 April 1957	Votipka, Elias, Tucker, Valentino Metropolitan Opera Orchestra & Chorus Cleva	Unpublished radio broadcast Met tour performance

Cavalleria rusticana/continued

New York 3 January 1959	Votipka, Elias, Barioni, Zanasi Metropolitan Opera Orchestra & Chorus Mitropoulos	CD: Hunt CDMP 472
New Orleans 14 December 1963	Cosenza, Kraft, Gismondo, Rayson New Orleans Opera Orchestra & Chorus Cellini	CD: VAI Audio VAIA 1053

Cavalleria rusticana, excerpt (Voi lo sapete)

Armed Forces Radio 1943		CD: Cantabile BIM 709 CD: Minerva MNA 15
New York 17 May 1945	Victor Orchestra Weissmann	78: Victor 11-8927 45: Victor 49-0291/WDM 1565/ERA 228 CD: RCA/BMG GD 60074
New York 7 July 1965		Unpublished radio broadcast
Trenton NJ 13 November 1966		CD: Cantabile BIM 709

Cavalleria rusticana, excerpt (Easter hymn)

New York 7 July 1965		CD: Cantabile BIM 709

WOLFGANG AMADEUS MOZART (1756-1791)

Don Giovanni

New York 3 April 1943	Role of Anna Novotna, Sayao, Melton, Pinza, Baccaloni, Harrell, Cordon Metropolitan Opera Orchestra & Chorus Breisach	CD: Walhall WHL 28 Excerpts LP: Ed Smith EJS 229 LP: Voce 118 CD: Legato BIM 709 CD: Minerva MNA 15 Legato and Minerva incorrectly described as San Francisco 1943

PAVCIC

The shepherdess

New York 15 October 1954	Kunc, piano	LP: Victor LM 1915

AMILCARE PONCHIELLI (1834-1886)

La Gioconda

New York 30 December 1939	Role of Gioconda Kaskas, Castagna, Martinelli, Morelli, Moscona Metropolitan Opera Orchestra & Chorus Panizza	LP: Ed Smith EJS 225 LP: Hope Records HOPE 201 CD: Myto MCD 914.42 CD: Symposium SYMCD 1176-1177 Excerpts LP: Ed Smith EJS 128/UORC 255
New York 16 March 1946	Harshaw, Stevens, Tucker, Warren, Vaghi Metropolitan Opera Orchestra & Chorus Cooper	CD: Myto MCD 952.127
New York 2 April 1955	S.Warfield, Rankin, Baum, Warren, Siepi Metropolitan Opera Orchestra & Chorus Cleva	Unpublished Met broadcast
New York 20 April 1957	Amparan, Rankin, Poggi, Warren, Siepi Metropolitan Opera Orchestra & Chorus Cleva	CD: Hunt CDMP 477 Excerpts LP: Gioielli della lirica GML 77 Complete opera probably also issued on LP
Rome July- August 1957	Amparan, Elias, Di Stefano, Warren, Clabassi Santa Cecilia Orchestra & Chorus Previtali	LP: Victor LM 6139/LSC 6139/ SB 2027-2030/VIC 6101/VICS 6101 LP: Decca D63 D3 LP: London OSA 13123 CD: Decca 444 5982 Excerpts LP: Victor LM 2249/LM 9903/LSC 9903 / LM 2709/LSC 2709

METROPOLITAN OPERA

SEASON 1956-1957

Thursday Evening, January 3, 1957, at 8:00

(Subscription Performance)

NEW PRODUCTION

ERNANI

An opera in a prologue and four acts
Libretto by F M. Piave
Based on the dram of Victor Hugo

Music by Giuseppe Verdi

Conductor: Dimitri Mitropoulos — Staged by Dino Yannopoulos

Sets and Costumes by Esteban Frances

Carlo, King of Spain	Frank Guarrera
Don Ruy Gomez De Silva	Giorgio Tozzi
Elvira	Zinka Milanov
Ernani	Mario Del Monaco
Don Riccardo	James McCracken
Jago	George Cehanovsky
Giovanna	Helen Vanni

Act IV:
Epithalamium

Choreography by Zachary Solov
Mary Ellen Moylan, Pierre Lacotte and Corps de Ballet

Chorus Master...... Kurt Adler
Associate Chorus Master..... Walter Taussig
Musical Preparation..... Victor Trucco

Program continued on the next page

IN THE EVENT OF AN AIR RAID ALARM REMAIN IN YOUR SEATS AND OBEY THE INSTRUCTIONS OF THE MANAGEMENT.—ROBERT L. CONDON, DIRECTOR OF CIVIL DEFENSE.

NOW ON RCA VICTOR RECORDS
Milanov, Bjoerling, Barbieri, Warren
IN VERDI'S
Il Trovatore
(COMPLETE)
ANOTHER SUPERB EXAMPLE OF
"THE Triple DIFFERENCE"
IN RCA VICTOR RECORDS
THE WORLD'S GREATEST
Artists
Today, as when Enrico Caruso first sang into the horn 50 years ago, "the world's greatest artists are on Victor Records."
THE WORLD'S TRUEST
Sound
RCA Victor, leader in the science of sound, today brings you "New Orthophonic Sound," with widest dynamic range.
THE WORLD'S FINEST
Quality
Rigid inspections in every step of manufacture, plus a new anti-static compound, assure clear and noise-free surfaces.
RCA
RCA VICTOR
...FIRST IN RECORDED MUSIC

La Gioconda, excerpts

New Orleans 5 November 1953	Madeira, Turner, Turrini, Bardelli, Moscona New Orleans Opera Orchestra & Chorus Herbert	CD: Legato SRO 814 CD: Cantabile BIM 709

La Gioconda, excerpt (Suicidio!)

New York 14 February 1946	Victor Orchestra Weissmann	78: Victor 11-9293 CD: RCA/BMG GD 60074
New York 21 May 1953	Victor Orchestra Cellini	LP: Victor LM 1777/VIC 1336/VICS 1336 LP: HMV ALP 1247 LP: Victor (Jugoslavia) LSRCA 70923 CD: Metropolitan Opera MET 107

GIACOMO PUCCINI (1858-1924)

La Bohème, excerpt (Donde lieta usci)

New York 18 September 1958	Victor Orchestra Basile	LP: Victor LM 2303/LSC 2303/VIC 1198/ VICS 1198 LP: Victor (Jugoslavia) LSRCA 70924 CD: RCA/BMG 09026 615802

Gianni Schicchi, excerpt (O mio babbino caro)

New York 18 September 1958	Victor Orchestra Basile	45: Victor ERA 9796 LP: Victor LM2303/LSC2303/VIC1198/VICS1198 LP: Victor (Jugoslavia) LSRCA 70924 CD: RCA/BMG GD 60074/09026 626892
Newark NJ 1965		CD: Cantabile BIM 709
Trenton NJ 13 November 1966		LP: MRF Records MRF 43 CD: Cantabile BIM 709

Madama Butterfly, excerpt (Un bel dì)

New York 23 September 1958	Victor Orchestra Basile	45: Victor ERA 9796 LP: Victor LM2303/LSC2303/VIC1198/VICS1198 LP: Victor (Jugoslavia) LSRCA 70924

Manon Lescaut, excerpt (In quelle trine morbide)

New York 18 September 1958	Victor Orchestra Basile	LP: Victor LM2303/LSC2303/VIC1198/VICS1198 LP: Victor (Jugoslavia) LSRCA 70924

Tosca

New York 4 April 1956	Role of Tosca Björling, Cassel Metropolitan Opera Orchestra & Chorus Mitropoulos	Unpublished private recording This was not a Met broadcast
London 1 July 1957	Corelli, Guelfi Covent Garden Orchestra & Chorus Gibson	LP: Ed Smith UORC 157 LP: Historical Recording Enterprises HRE 336 CD: Legato SRO 511 Excerpts LP: Legendary LR 186 CD: Legato BIM 709
Rome 2-18 July 1957	Björling, Warren Rome Opera Orchestra & Chorus Leinsdorf	LP: Victor LM 6052/LSC 6052/ RB 16051-16052/VIC 6000/ VICS 6000/VL 43535 CD: RCA/BMG 84514 Excerpts 45: Victor ERA 9796 LP: Victor LM 9811/LM 2570/LSC 9811/ LSC 2570/VICS 1740 LP: RCA (Germany) KR 11041 CD: Metropolitan Opera MET 107 CD: RCA/BMG GD 60192 This version of Tosca also published unofficially on CD by Historical Performers

ROBERT SCHUMANN (1810-1856)

Mondnacht

New York 15 October 1954	Kunc, piano	LP: Victor LM 1915

Widmung

New York 15 October 1954	Kunc, piano	LP: Victor LM 1915

RICHARD STRAUSS (1864-1949)

Allerseelen

New York 15 October 1954	Kunc, piano	LP: Victor LM 1915
Newark NJ 1965		CD: Legato BIM 709

Cäcilie

New York 15 October 1954	Kunc, piano	LP: Victor LM 1915

Freundliche Vision

New York 15 October 1954	Kunc, piano	LP: Victor LM 1915

Zueignung

New York 15 October 1954	Kunc, piano	LP: Victor LM 1915 CD: RCA/BMG GD 60074
Newark NJ 1965		CD: Legato BIM 709

GIUSEPPE VERDI (1813-1901)

Aida

New York 26 February 1938	Role of Aida Castagna, Martinelli/Jagel, Tagliabue Metropolitan Opera Orchestra & Chorus Papi	Unpublished Met broadcast Excerpts LP: Ed Smith UORC 262
New York 4 February 1939	Castagna, Gigli, Tagliabue Metropolitan Opera Orchestra & Chorus Panizza	Unpublished Met broadcast Excerpts LP: Ed Smith EJS 485 LP: MRF Records MRF 43 CD: Great Opera Performances GOP 804
New York 6 March 1943	Castagna, Martinelli, Bonelli, Condon Metropolitan Opera Orchestra & Chorus Pelletier	LP: Ed Smith EJS 500 LP: Cetra LO 26 CD: Great Opera Performances GOP 784 Excerpts LP: Ed Smith EJS 236
New York 8 March 1952	Rankin, Del Monaco, Warren, Hines Metropolitan Opera Orchestra & Chorus Cleva	LP: Ed Smith UORC 325 CD: Myto MCD 953.129
New York 24 January 1953	Thebom, Del Monaco, London, Hines Metropolitan Opera Orchestra & Chorus Cleva	Unpublished Met broadcast
Rome 2-18 July 1955	Barbieri, Björling, Warren, Christoff Rome Opera Orchestra & Chorus Perlea	LP: Victor LM 6122/VIC 6119/VL 43533 LP: HMV ALP 1388-1390 CD: RCA/BMG GD 86652 Excerpts 45: HMV 7ER 5041 LP: Victor LM 2046/LM 2628/LM 2736/ LM 6061/LM 6069/RB 6516/RB 6585/ RB 16089/SER 5704-5706/AVL1-0906/ RL 43077/RL 43243 CD: RCA/BMG GD 87799

Aida, excerpt (Ritorna vincitor!)

New York 14 February 1946	Victor Orchestra Weissmann	78: Victor 11-9839/11-9288 LP: Metropolitan Opera MET 404
New York 1947	Firestone Orchestra	CD: Legato BIM 709
New York 18 May 1953	Victor Orchestra Cellini	45: Victor ERB 19 LP: Victor LM 1777/LM 6171/ VIC 1336/VICS 1336 LP: HMV ALP 1247 LP: Victor (Jugoslavia) LSRCA 70923 CD: Metropolitan Opera MET 107

Aida, excerpt (O patria mia)

New York 18 May 1953	Victor Orchestra Cellini	45: Victor ERB 19 LP: Victor LM 1777/VIC 1336/VICS 1336 LP: HMV ALP 1247 LP: Victor (Jugoslavia) LSRCA 70923 CD: Metropolitan Opera MET 107

Un ballo in maschera

New York 14 December 1940	Role of Amelia Andreva, Castagna, Björling, Sved Metropolitan Opera Orchestra & Chorus Panizza	LP: Ed Smith EJS 230 LP: Historical Operatic Treasures ERR 109 LP: Rococo 1003 LP: Robin Hood RHR 516 LP: Metropolitan Opera Guild MET 8 CD: Myto MCD 90.317 Excerpts CD: Radio Years RY 12 CD: Minerva MNA 15
New York 15 January 1944	Greer, Thorborg, Peerce, Warren Metropolitan Opera Orchestra & Chorus Walter	LP: Discocorp BWS 805 CD: 40s Label FTO 31112
New York 22 January 1955	Peters, Madeira, Tucker, Metternich Metropolitan Opera Orchestra & Chorus Mitropoulos	LP: Raritas OPR 408 LP: Cetra LO 4 LP: Foyer FO 1020 CD: Foyer 2CF-2004 Excerpts LP: Gioielli della lirica GML 13
New York 10 December 1955	Peters, Anderson, Peerce, Merrill Metropolitan Opera Orchestra & Chorus Mitropoulos	CD: Myto MCD 942.100

Queen's Hall

Sole Lessees: Messrs. Chappell and Co., Ltd.

London Music Festival

FOURTH CONCERT

Monday 30 May 1938 at 8.15 p.m.

Te Deum, for Double Chorus and Orchestra — VERDI 1813—1901

INTERVAL

Requiem Mass, for Four Solo Voices, Chorus and Orchestra — VERDI

Zinka Milanov
Kerstin Thorborg
Helge Roswaenge
Nicola Moscona

The B.B.C. Choral Society
(Chorus Master: Leslie Woodgate)

The B.B.C. Symphony Orchestra
Leader: Paul Beard — Organ: Berkeley Mason

CONDUCTOR: Arturo Toscanini

METROPOLITAN OPERA

SEASON 1952-1953

Thursday Evening, December 4, 1952, at 8:00

(Subscription Performance)

New Production

LA FORZA DEL DESTINO

(The Power of Destiny)

Opera in three acts

Libretto by F. M. Piave

Music by Giuseppe Verdi

Conductor: Fritz Stiedry — Staged by Herbert Graf

Decor and Costumes by Eugene Berman

The Marquis of Calatrava	Lubomir Vichegonov
Leonora, his daughter	Zinka Milanov
Don Carlo, her brother	Giuseppe Valdengo
Don Alvaro	Mario Del Monaco
Padre Guardiano	Cesare Siepi
Fra Melitone	Gerhard Pechner
Preziosilla, a camp-follower	Mildred Miller
Curra, Leonora's maid	Laura Castellano
A Surgeon	Algerd Brazis

Chorus Master . . . . Kurt Adler

Assistant Chorus Master . . . Walter Taussig

Choreography by Zachary Solov

Program continued on the next page

IN THE EVENT OF AN AIR RAID ALARM REMAIN IN YOUR SEATS AND OBEY THE INSTRUCTIONS OF THE MANAGEMENT.—ARTHUR H. WALLANDER, DIRECTOR OF CIVIL DEFENSE.

Un ballo in maschera, scenes

New York 21 January 1955	Peters, Anderson, Peerce, Warren Metropolitan Opera Orchestra & Chorus Mitropoulos	LP: Victor LM 1911/LM 1932/LM 20146 LP: HMV ALP 1476 LP: Melodiya D 013891 CD: RCA/BMG RG 79112 CD: Theorema TH 121.146 Excerpts LP: Victor VIC 1336/VICS 1336 CD: RCA/BMG GD 60074/GD 87911/ CD: Metropolitan Opera MET 107

Un ballo in maschera, excerpt (Ecco l'orrido campo!)

Armed Forces Radio 1943		CD: Cantabile BIM 709 CD: Minerva MNA 15

Ernani

New York 29 December 1956	Role of Elvira Del Monaco, Warren, Siepi Metropolitan Opera Orchestra & Chorus Mitropoulos	LP: MRF Records MRF 6 LP: Cetra LO 12 LP: Foyer FO 1026 LP: Dei della musica DMV 17-19 CD: Foyer 2CF-2006 CD: Hunt CDMP 470

La forza del destino

New York 29 November 1952	Role of Leonora Miller, Tucker, Warren, Hines, Pechner Metropolitan Opera Orchestra & Chorus Stiedry	CD: Music and Arts CD 693
New Orleans 12-14 March 1953	Turner, Del Monaco, Warren, Widermann, Pechner New Orleans Opera Orchestra & Chorus Herbert	LP: Ed Smith UORC 222 CD: Legato LCD 118 Excerpt LP: Voce 97 CD: Legato BIM 709
New York 20 March 1954	Madeira, Penno, Warren, Hines, Pechner Metropolitan Opera Orchestra & Chorus Stiedry	Unpublished Met broadcast
New York 17 March 1956	Elias, Tucker, Warren, Siepi, Corena Metropolitan Opera Orchestra & Chorus Stiedry	LP: Movimento musica 03.028 CD: Myto MCD 943.106
Rome August 1957	Elias, Di Stefano, Warren, Tozzi, Montavani Santa Cecilia Orchestra & Chorus Previtali	LP: Victor LM 6406/LSC 6406/ RE 25016-25019/SER 4516-4519 LP: Decca GOM 660-662/GOS 660-662 CD: Decca 443 6782 Excerpts LP: Victor LM 9877/LM 2709/LSC 2709 LP: Decca GOS 666-668

La forza del destino, excerpt (Ma pellegrina ed orfano!)

New York 18 May 1953	Victor Orchestra Cellini	LP: Victor LM 1916 LP: HMV ALP 1371
New York 19 October 1954	NBC SO Perlea	Victor unpublished

La forza del destino, excerpt (Madre pietosa vergine)

New York 21 May 1953	Victor Orchestra Shaw Chorale Cellini	45: HMV 7ER 5032 LP: Victor LM 1916/LM 2269/LM 1777/ VIC 1336/VICS 1336 LP: HMV ALP 1371/ALP 1427 LP: Victor (Jugoslavia) LSRCA 70923 LP: Metropolitan Opera MET 405 CD: Metropolitan Opera MET 107

La forza del destino, excerpt (La vergine degli angeli)

New York 21 May 1953	Vichegonov Victor Orchestra Shaw Chorale Cellini	45: HMV 7ER 5032 LP: Victor LM 1916/LM 2269/LM 1777/ VIC 1336/VICS 1336 LP: HMV ALP 1371/ALP 1427 LP: Victor (Jugoslavia) LSRCA 70923 CD: Metropolitan Opera MET 107
New York 7 July 1965		CD: Legato BIM 709

La forza del destino, excerpt (Pace pace, mio Dio!)

New York 17 May 1945	Victor Orchestra Weissmann	78: Victor 11-8927/M 1474 45: Victor 49-0291/WDM 1474/12-3066 LP: Victor VICS 6044 LP: EMI EX 29 10753 CD: RCA/BMG GD 60074
New York 6 April 1953	ABC SO Cleva	Unpublished video recording First ever Met simulcast
New York 18 May 1953	Victor Orchestra Cellini	45: Victor ERA 206 45: HMV 7ER 5032 LP: Victor LM 1777/LM 1847/LM 1909/ LM 1916/LM 2269/VIC 1336/VICS 1336 LP: HMV ALP 1371/ALP 1427 LP: Victor (Jugoslavia) LSRCA 70923 CD: Metropolitan Opera MET 107
New York 7 July 1965		CD: Legato BIM 709
Newark NJ 1965		CD: Legato BIM 709

La forza del destino, excerpt (Io muoio!/Non imprecare!)

New York 7 April 1955	Peerce, Warren, Moscona Victor Orchestra Cellini	LP: Victor LM 1916/VIC 1336/VICS 1336 LP: HMV ALP 1371 CD: RCA/BMG GD 60074

Otello

New York 21 November 1964	Role of Desdemona Grillo, Uzunov, J.Alexander, MacNeil Metropolitan Opera Orchestra & Chorus Schippers	Unpublished Met broadcast Excerpts LP: MRF Records MRF 84

Otello, excerpt (Piangea cantando)

New York 25 September 1958	Elias Victor Orchestra Basile	LP: Victor LM2303/LSC2303/VIC1198/VICS1198 LP: Victor (Jugoslavia) LSRCA 70924 CD: Metropolitan Opera MET 514
New York 20 November 1963	Metropolitan Opera Orchestra Schick	LP: MRF Records MRF 43 Gala performance for Giovanni Martinelli
Trenton NJ 13 November 1966		CD: Legato BIM 709

Otello, excerpt (Ave Maria)

New York 18 September 1958	Victor Orchestra Basile	LP: Victor LM2303/LSC2303/VIC1198/VICS1198 LP: Victor (Jugoslavia) LSRCA 70924 CD: Metropolitan Opera MET 107
New York 20 November 1963	Metropolitan Opera Orchestra Schick	LP: MRF Records MRF 43 Gala performance for Giovanni Martinelli
Trenton NJ 13 November 1966		CD: Legato BIM 709

Rigoletto, Act 4

New York 25 May 1944	Role of Gilda Merriman, Peerce, Warren, Moscona NBC SO Toscanini	LP: Victor LM 6041/RB 16140/VIC 1314/ AT 304/AT 1048/VCM 6/VCM 10/ VL 46005 LP: HMV ALP 1453 LP: Laudis 1002 LP: Franklin Mint LP: Movimento musica 01.002 CD: Movimento musica 011.008 CD: RCA/BMG GD 60276 CD: Memories HR 4188-4189 Excerpts CD: Radio Years RY 12 CD: Minerva MNA 15

Simon Boccanegra

New York 2 April 1960	Role of Amelia Bergonzi, Guarrera, Tozzi, Flagello, Scott Metropolitan Opera Orchestra & Chorus Mitropoulos	LP: MRF Records MRF 84 LP: Estro armonico EA 023 LP: Foyer FO 1023 CD: Stradivarius STR 10032-10033 CD: Memories HR 4539-4540 CD: Discantus (Greece) 189 6492

Il trovatore

New York 4 March 1939	Role of Leonora Castagna, Martinelli, Bonelli Metropolitan Opera Orchestra & Chorus Papi	Unpublished Met broadcast Excerpts LP: Ed Smith EJS 512/ANNA 1030 ANNA 1030 may have been incorrectly dated January 1939
New York 31 March 1945	Castagna, Baum, Warren, Moscona Metropolitan Opera Orchestra & Chorus Sodero	CD: Walhall WHL 36 Excerpts LP: Ed Smith EJS 130 EJS 130 incorrectly dated 1938-1939
New York February- March 1952	Barbieri, Björling, Warren, Moscona Victor Orchestra Shaw Chorale Cellini	45: Victor WDM 6008 LP: Victor LM 6008/AVM2-0699/VL 43536 LP: HMV ALP 1112-1113/ALP 1832-1833 LP: Melodiya D 033317-033322 CD: RCA/BMG GD 86643 Excerpts LP: Victor LM 1827/LM 2736/ RB 6585/RB 16089 LP: Ed Smith EJS 130 CD: RCA/BMG GD 87799 EJS 130 incorrectly dated 1938
New York 16 January 1954	Nikolaidi, Baum, Warren, Moscona Metropolitan Opera Orchestra & Chorus Cleva	Unpublished Met broadcast
New York 14 April 1956	Rankin, Baum, Warren, Tozzi Metropolitan Opera Orchestra & Chorus Cleva	LP: Melodram MEL 009 LP: Dei della musica DMV 23-25 LP: Sonata 9064

Il trovatore, excerpt (D'amor sull' ali rosee)

New York 17 May 1945- 14 February 1946	Victor Orchestra Weissmann	78: Victor 11-9839 78: HMV DB 6877 CD: RCA/BMG GD 60074 2 different takes of the aria used
New York 2 May 1951	Victor Orchestra Cellini	45: Victor 49-3739 LP: Victor LM 1777/VIC 1336/VICS 1336 LP: HMV ALP 1247 LP: Victor (Jugoslavia) LSRCA 70923 CD: Metropolitan Opera MET 107

Il trovatore, excerpt (Tacea la notte placida)

New York 14 February 1945- 14 February 1946	Victor Orchestra Weissmann	78: Victor 11-9839 78: HMV DB 6877 LP: Victor VICS 6044 LP: EMI EX 769 7411 CD: EMI CHS 769 7412
New York 2 May 1951	Victor Orchestra Cellini	45: Victor 49-3739/ERA 228 LP: Victor LM 1777/VIC 1336/VICS 1336 LP: HMV ALP 1247 LP: Victor (Jugoslavia) LSRCA 70923 CD: Metropolitan Opera MET 107

Il trovatore, excerpt (Quel son! Quelle preci!)

New York 16 April 1945	Peerce Victor Orchestra and Chorus Weissmann	78: Victor 11-8782 45: Victor 49-0129 LP: Victor VICS 6044 CD: Victor GD 60074
New York 9 May 1951	Peerce Victor Orchestra Shaw Chorale Cellini	45: Victor 49-3740

Il trovatore, excerpt (Udiste? Come albeggi/Conte! Nè basti!)

New York 9 May- December 1951	Warren Victor Orchestra Cellini	45: Victor 49-3740

A recorded performance of the Miserere from Il trovatore, performed by Milanov and Peerce and conducted by S.Levin, has been mentioned by some commentators

Requiem

New York 4 March 1938	Castagna, Kullmann, Moscona NBC SO Westminster Choir Toscanini	CD: Legato LCD 178
London 27 May 1938	Thorborg, Rosvaenge, Moscona BBC SO BBC Chorus Toscanini	LP: Vocal Art LP: MKR Records MKR 1001-1002 LP: Ed Smith UORC 108 LP: Toscanini Society ATS 1108-1109 CD: Melodram MEL 28022 Excerpts CD: Radio Years RY 12 CD: Cantabile BIM 709 CD: Minerva MNA 15
New York 23 November 1940	Castagna, Björling, Moscona NBC SO Westminster Choir Toscanini	LP: Ed Smith UORC 229 LP: Toscanini Society ATS 1005-1006 LP: Melodram MEL 006 LP: Turnabout THS 65031-65032 CD: Music and Arts ATRA 240 CD: Melodram MEL 38006 CD: Palette (Japan) PAL 3004-3006 CD: Greenline 3CLC 4003
New York 29 March 1959	Elias, Bergonzi, Tozzi Metropolitan Opera Orchestra & Chorus Walter	CD: As-Disc AS 408 Not a Met broadcast; Milanov withdraws from performance after Dies irae and replaced by Krall

JUGOSLAV SONGS

No bembasi; U kor; Daleko memoi Split; Domovini Ljubavi; Gor' caz jezero; Ko lani sem

1943	Orchestra Goranin	LP: Halo 50281 LP: Robin Hood RHR 516 CD: Legato BIM 709 CD: Minerva MNA 15

MILANOV INTERVIEWS

Discussion of her singing and career

1976-1978	CD: Cantabile BIM 709

Interview with Peter Grevina

15 April 1966	Unpublished radio broadcast

Leontyne Price
born 1927

with additional assistance from Michael Gray

Discography compiled
by John Hunt

ADOLPHE ADAM (1803-1856)

O holy night, arranged by Totzauer

Vienna 3-5 June 1961	VPO Karajan	45: Decca CEP 729/SEC 5112 LP: Decca LXT 5657/SXL 2294/JB 38 LP: London 5644/OSA 25280 CD: Decca 421 1032/448 9982

HAROLD ARLEN (1905-1986)

A sleepin' bee

Los Angeles 9-11 May 1967	Orchestra Previn	LP: Victor LM 2983/LSC 2983/ARL1-1029

Right as the rain

Los Angeles 9-11 May 1967	Orchestra Previn	LP: Victor LM 2983/LSC 2983/ARL1-1029

JOHANN SEBASTIAN BACH (1685-1750)

Mass in B minor

Salzburg 20 August 1961	C.Ludwig, Gedda, Souzay, Berry Wiener Singverein VPO Karajan	LP: Movimento musica 03.012

Ave Maria, arranged by Gounod and Sabatini

Vienna 3-5 June 1961	VPO Karajan	45: Decca CEP 729/SEC 5112 LP: Decca LXT 5657/SXL 2294/JB 38 LP: London 5644/OSA 25280 CD: Decca 421 1032/448 9982

Ave Maria, arranged by Hayman

New York 21 May 1969	Orchestra Fiedler	LP: Victor PRS 288 CD: RCA/BMG 09026 681532

Vom Himmel hoch, arranged by Meyer

Vienna 3-5 June 1961	VPO Karajan	LP: Decca LXT 5657/SXL 2294/JB 38 LP: London 5644/OSA 25280 CD: Decca 421 1032/448 9982

SAMUEL BARBER (1910-1981)

Antony and Cleopatra

New York 16 September 1966	Role of Cleopatra Elias, J.Thomas, Diaz, Flagello, Metropolitan Opera Orchestra & Chorus Schippers	Unpublished Met broadcast Premiere performances of the work

Antony and Cleopatra, excerpt (Give me some music)

Walthamstow 1-2 June 1968	New Philharmonia Schippers	LP: Victor LSC 3062/SB 6799 CD: RCA/BMG 09026 619832

Antony and Cleopatra, excerpt (Give me my robe)

Paris 15 February 1968	Orchestre National Rizchin	CD: Hunt CDGI 803
Walthamstow 1-2 June 1968	New Philharmonia Schippers	LP: Victor LSC 3062/SB 6799/RL 85177 LP: Metropolitan Opera MET 104 CD: RCA/BMG 09026 615802/09026 619832/ 09026 681532

Vanessa, excerpt (He has come)

Rome 2-6 August 1965	RCA Italiana Orchestra Molinari-Pradelli	LP: Victor LM 2898/LSC 2898/ RB 6700/SB 6700 CD: RCA/BMG 09026 612362/09026 681532

Knoxville Summer of 1915, for soprano and orchestra

Walthamstow 1-2 June 1968	New Philharmonia Schippers	LP: Victor LSC 3062/SB 6799 CD: RCA/BMG 09026 681532

Hermit songs

Washington 30 October 1953	Barber, piano	LP: Columbia ML 4988 CD: Sony MPK 46727 CD: RCA/BMG 09026 619832

LUDWIG VAN BEETHOVEN (1770-1827)

Fidelio, excerpt (Abscheulicher, wo eilst du hin?)

Walthamstow 9-23 July 1970	LSO Cleva	LP: Victor LM 3218/LSC 3218/SER 5621 CD: RCA/BMG 09026 681532

Missa solemnis

Salzburg 19 August 1959	C.Ludwig, Gedda, Zaccaria Wiener Singverein VPO Karajan	LP: Melodram MEL 704 CD: Nuova Era NE 2262-2263

Symphony No 9 "Choral"

Boston 21-22 December 1958	Forrester, Poleri, Tozzi Boston SO Münch	LP: Victor LM 6006/LSC 6006/VIC 1114/ VICS 1114/VICS 1660/VICS 6003

VINCENZO BELLINI (1801-1835)

Norma, excerpt (Casta diva)

Walthamstow 1-8 August 1979	Martinovich Philharmonia Ambrosian Singers H.Lewis	LP: RCA ARL1-3522 CD: RCA/BMG 09026 612362

Norma, excerpt (Mira o Norma!)

New York 28 March 1982	Horne Metropolitan Opera Orchestra Levine	CD: RCA/BMG 09026 681532 Also unpublished video recording

HECTOR BERLIOZ (1803-1869)

La damnation de Faust, excerpt (D'amour l'ardente flamme)

Walthamstow 7-15 July 1977	New Philharmonia Santi	LP: RCA ARL1-2529 CD: RCA/BMG 09026 612362

Les nuits d'été

Chicago 4 March 1963	Chicago SO Reiner	LP: Victor LM 2695/LSC 2695/ RB 6566/SB 6566 CD: RCA/BMG RD 61234/09026 681532 L'absence CD: RCA/BMG 09026 681522

Vilanelle/Les nuits d'été

New York 26 January 1991	Garvey. piano	CD: RCA/BMG 09026 684352

LEONARD BERNSTEIN (1918-1990)

West Side Story, excerpt (Somewhere)

New York 8 November 1987	Orchestra Bernstein	CD: DG 429 3922

GEORGES BIZET (1838-1875)

Carmen

Vienna August 1962- November 1963	Role of Carmen Freni, Corelli, Merrill Vienna Opera Chorus VPO Karajan	LP: Victor LD 6164/LDS 6164/LMDS 6199/ LSC 6199/SER 5600-5602/VL 45477/ EX 26.35035 CD: RCA/BMG GD 86199/74321 394952 Excerpts LP: Victor LM 2843/LSC 2843/LSC 3341/ RB 6671/SB 6671/RL 42427 CD: RCA/BMG GD 60190/09026 681522/ 09026 681532 Unofficial CD issue of complete opera also on Lyrica LRC 01013

Carmen, excerpt (Je dis que rien ne m'épouvante)

Walthamstow 13-18 July 1969	LSO Downes	LP: Victor LSC 3163/SER 5589 CD: RCA/BMG 09026 612362

EDWARD BOATNER

On ma journey, arranged by Paur

New York 7-18 December 1961	Orchestra and Chorus Paur	LP: Victor LM 2600/LSC 2600 CD: RCA/BMG 09026 681532

JERRY BOCK (Born 1928)

Sunrise sunset

Los Angeles 9-11 May 1967	Orchestra Previn	LP: Victor LM 2983/LSC 2983/ARL1-1029

HENRY BURLEIGH (1866-1949)

Ev'ry time I feel the spirit, arranged by Paur

New York 7-18 December 1961	Orchestra and Chorus Paur	LP: Victor LM 2600/LSC 2600 CD: RCA/BMG 09026 681532

Let us cheer the weary traveller, arranged by Vene

New York 19-22 April 1970	Rust College Choir Holmes	LP: Victor LM 3183/LSC 3183 CD: RCA/BMG 09026 681532

BURNETT

My melancholy baby

Los Angeles 9-11 May 1967	Previn, piano Manne Brown	LP: Victor LM 2983/LSC 2983/ARL1-1029

GUSTAVE CHARPENTIER (1860-1950)

Louise, excerpt (Depuis le jour)

Rome 2-6 August 1965	RCA Italiana Orchestra Molinari-Pradelli	LP: Victor LM 2898/LSC 2898/ RB 6700/SB 6700 CD: RCA/BMG 09026 612362
Munich 27 January 1968	Bavarian RO Franci	CD: Gala GL 328

ARRIGO BOITO (1842-1918)

Mefistofele, excerpt (L'altra notte)

Rome 24-28 June 1967	RCA Italiana Orchestra Molinari-Pradelli	LP: Victor LM 2968/LSC 2968/SB 6742 CD: RCA/BMG 09026 612362

MAY BRAHE (1885-1956)

Bless this house

New York 4-7 April 1966	St.Thomas Choir Self	LP: Victor LM 2918/LSC 2918 CD: RCA/BMG 09026 681532

JOHANNES BRAHMS (1833-1897)

Zigeunerlieder

New York 28 February 1965	Garvey, piano	CD: RCA/BMG 09026 681532

BENJAMIN BRITTEN (1913-1976)

Gloriana, excerpt (O God my king, sole ruler of the world)

Walthamstow 1-8 August 1979	Philharmonia H.Lewis	LP: RCA ARL1-3522 CD: RCA/BMG 09026 612362

SALZBURGER FESTSPIELE 1959

ACHTES ORCHESTER-KONZERT

DIE WIENER PHILHARMONIKER

DER SINGVEREIN DER GESELLSCHAFT DER MUSIKFREUNDE IN WIEN

unter der Leitung von

HERBERT VON KARAJAN

Solisten

LEONTYNE PRICE

CHRISTA LUDWIG

NICOLAI GEDDA

NICOLA ZACCARIA

SALZBURGER FESTSPIELE 1960

40 JAHRE SALZBURGER FESTSPIELE

ACHTES ORCHESTER-KONZERT

WOLFGANG AMADEUS MOZART

REQUIEM

für Soli, Chor, Orchester und Orgel

ANTON BRUCKNER

TE DEUM

für Soli, Chor, Orchester und Orgel

Solisten
LEONTYNE PRICE
HILDE RÖSSEL- MAJDAN
FRITZ WUNDERLICH
WALTER BERRY
EBERHARD WÄCHTER

DIRIGENT
HERBERT VON KARAJAN

DIE WIENER PHILHARMONIKER
DER SINGVEREIN DER GESELLSCHAFT DER MUSIKFREUNDE WIEN

FRANCESCO CILEA (1866-1950)

Adriana Lecouvreur, excerpt (Io son L'umila ancella)

New York 28 February 1965	Garvey, piano	CD: RCA/BMG 09026 681532
Rome 2-6 August 1965	RCA Italiana Orchestra Molinari-Pradelli	LP: Victor LM 2898/LSC 2898/ RB 6700/SB 6700 CD: RCA/BMG 09026 612362
New York 1 January 1967	Bell Telephone Orchestra Voshees	CD: Great Operatic Performances GOP 736
Paris 15 February 1968	Orchestre National Rizchin	CD: Hunt CDGI 803
San Francisco 23 January 1973	San Francisco SO Ozawa	CD: Gala GL 328
Saint Paul 8 January 1985	Garvey, piano	LP: Pro Arte PAD 231 CD: Pro Arte CDD 231
New York 26 January 1991	Garvey, piano	CD: RCA/BMG 09026 684532

Adriana Lecouvreur, excerpt (Poveri fiori)

Walthamstow 7-15 July 1977	New Philharmonia Santi	LP: RCA ARL1-2529 CD: RCA/BMG 09026 612362

CHARLES CONVERSE

What a friend we have in Jesus

New York 4-7 April 1966	St.Thomas Choir Self	LP: Victor LM 2918/LSC 2918 CD: RCA/BMG 09026 681532

CLAUDE DEBUSSY (1862-1918)

L'enfant prodigue, excerpt (Air de Lia)

Rome 24-28 June 1967	RCA Italiana Orchestra Molinari-Pradelli	LP: Victor LM 2968/LSC 2968/SB 6742 CD: RCA/BMG 09026 612362
San Francisco 23 January 1973	San Francisco SO Ozawa	CD: Gala GL 328

WILLIAM DOANE (1832-1915)

Pass me not, o gentle saviour

New York 4-7 April 1966	St.Thomas Choir Self	LP: Victor LM 2918/LSC 2918 CD: RCA/BMG 09026 681532

TOMMY DORSEY

When I've done my best

New York 16 March 1971	Swann, organ	LP: Victor LM 3219/LSC 3219

HENRI DUPARC (1848-1933)

Extase

New York 26 January 1971	Garvey, piano	CD: RCA/BMG 09026 684352

ANTONIN DVORAK (1841-1904)

Rusalka, excerpt (O silver moon)

Walthamstow 7-15 July 1977	New Philharmonia Santi	LP: RCA ARL1-2529 CD: RCA/BMG 09026 612362

JOHN DYKES (1823-1876)

Holy holy holy!; Lead kindly light

New York 4-7 April 1966	St.Thomas Choir Self	LP: Victor LM 2918/LSC 2918 CD: RCA/BMG 09026 681532

MANUEL DE FALLA (1876-1946)

El amor brujo

Chicago 4 March 1963	Chicago SO Reiner	LP: Victor LM 2695/LSC 2695/ RB 6566/SB 6566 CD: RCA/BMG RD 85404/09026 625862

GABRIEL FAURE (1845-1924)

Mélodies: Clair de lune; Notre amour; Au cimetière; Au bord de l'eau; Mandoline

New York 11 April 1958- 9 January 1959	Garvey, piano	LP: Victor LM 2279/LSC 2279 CD: RCA/BMG 09026 614992/09026 681532

FRIEDRICH FLOTOW (1812-1883)

Martha, excerpt (The last rose of summer)

Walthamstow 13-18 July 1969	LSO Downes	LP: Victor LSC 3163/SER 5589 CD: RCA/BMG 09026 612362

GEORGE GERSHWIN (1898-1937)

Porgy and Bess, scenes

New York 13-17 May 1963	Role of Bess W.Warfield, Bubbles, Boatwright Victor Orchestra and Chorus Henderson	LP: Victor LM 2679/LSC 2679/RB 6552/ SB 6552/GL 42149 CD: RCA/BMG GD 85234/74321 242182 Excerpts CD: RCA/BMG 09026 681522/09026 681532

Porgy and Bess, excerpt (Summertime)

New York 6 April 1953	ABC SO Rudolf	Unpublished video recording Price's first appearance at Metropolitan; first ever Met radio and TV simulcast
1960	Instrumental ensemble	LP: Decca MET 201-203/SET 201-203/ D247 D3/EK 635.107/GRV 10 CD: Decca 421 0462/440 4022/440 6542 Insert for gala sequence in Decca's Karajan Fledermaus recording
Munich 27 January 1968	Bavarian RO Franci	CD: Gala GL 328
Paris 15 February 1968	Orchestre National Rizchin	CD: Hunt CDGI 803
Saint Paul 8 January 1985	Garvey, piano	LP: Pro Arte PAD 231 CD: Pro Arte CDD 231
New York 26 January 1991	Garvey, piano	CD: RCA/BMG 09026 684352

Love walked in

Los Angeles 9-11 May 1967	Previn, piano Manne Brown	LP: Victor LM 2983/LSC 2983/ARL1-1029

UMBERTO GIORDANO (1867-1948)

Andrea Chenier, excerpt (La mamma morta)

Rome 24-28 June 1967	RCA Italiana Orchestra Molinari-Pradelli	LP: Victor LM 2968/LSC 2968/SB 6742 CD: RCA/BMG 09026 612362

CHRISTOPH WILLIBALD GLUCK (1714-1787)

Alceste, excerpt (Divinités du Styx!)

Walthamstow 13-18 July 1969	LSO Downes	LP: Victor LSC 3163/SER 5589 CD: RCA/BMG 09026 612362

FRANZ XAVER GRUBER (1787-1863)

Stille Nacht heilige Nacht

Vienna 3-5 June 1961	Wiener Singverein VPO Karajan	LP: Decca LXT 5657/SXL 2294/JB 38 LP: London 5644/OSA 25280 CD: Decca 421 1032/448 9982

REYNALDO HAHN (1875-1947)

Le printemps

Saint Paul 8 January 1985	Garvey, piano	LP: Pro Arte PAD 231 CD: Pro Arte CDD 231
New York 26 January 1991	Garvey, piano	CD: RCA/BMG 09026 684352

HALL JOHNSON

His name is so sweet, arranged by Paur

New York 7-18 December 1961	Orchestra and Chorus Paur	LP: Victor LM 2600/LSC 2600 CD: RCA/BMG 09026 681532

Honor honor!, arranged by Paur

New York 7-18 December 1961	Orchestra and Chorus Paur	LP: Victor LM 2600/LSC 2600 CD: RCA/BMG 09026 681532

Ride on King Jesus!

New York 7-18 December 1961	Orchestra and Chorus Paur	LP: Victor LM 2600/LSC 2600 CD: RCA/BMG 09026 681532/09026 681522 Arrangement by Paur
Saint Paul 8 January 1985	Garvey, piano	LP: Pro Arte PAD 231 CD: Pro Arte CDD 231
New York 26 January 1991	Garvey, piano	CD: RCA/BMG 09026 684352

Witness

New York 26 January 1991	Garvey, piano	CD: RCA/BMG 09026 684352

GEORGE FRIDERIC HANDEL (1685-1759)

Atalanta, excerpt (Care selve)

Rome 24-28 June 1967	RCA Italiana Orchestra Molinari-Pradelli	LP: Victor LM 2968/LSC 2968/SB 6742 CD: RCA/BMG 09026 612362

Giulio Cesare, excerpt (Da tempeste il legno infranto)

New York 9 October 1956	American Opera Society Orchestra Garrison	CD: Hunt CDGI 803

Giulio Cesare, excerpt (Piangerò la sorte mia)

New York 9 October 1956	American Opera Society Orchestra Garrison	CD: Hunt CDGI 803

Giulio Cesare, excerpt (Se pietà di me non senti)

New York 9 October 1956	American Opera Society Orchestra Garrison	CD: Hunt CDGI 803
New York 26 January 1991	Garvey, piano	CD: RCA/BMG 09026 684352

Robert Paterson presents

Leontyne Price

London Symphony Orchestra

Leader: John Georgiadis

Mario Bernardi

ROYAL ALBERT HALL

General Manager: F. J. MUNDY

Sunday, 16th June 1968

Programme

Don Giovanni, Overture	Mozart
Le Nozze di Figaro—act 3: *E Susanna non vien—Dove sono*	Mozart
Ernani—act 1 : *Surta e la notte—Ernani, Ernani involami*	Verdi
Alborada del Gracioso	Ravel
Louise—act 3: *Depuis le Jour*	Charpentier
Manon—act 2: *Allons! il le faut!—Adieu notre petite table*	Massenet

INTERVAL

L'Italiana in Algeri (The Italian Girl in Algiers), Overture	Rossini
Suor Angelica—*Senza mamma*	Puccini
Adrianna Lecouvreur—act 1: *Io son l'umille ancella*	Cilea
Rosamunde, Overture (D 644)	Schubert
La Forza del Destino—act 4: *Pace, pace mio Dio*	Verdi

Giulio Cesare, excerpt (Tu la mia stella sei)

New York 9 October 1956	American Opera Society Orchestra Garrison	CD: Hunt CDGI 803

Giulio Cesare, excerpt (V'adoro pupille)

Berlin 18 September 1960	BPO Karajan	LP: Legendary LR 139

Rinaldo, excerpt (Fermate!)

New York 28 March 1982	Horne Metropolitan Opera Orchestra Levine	Unpublished radio broadcast and unpublished video recording

Semele, excerpt (Wher'er you walk)

Walthamstow 1-8 August 1979	Philharmonia H.Lewis	LP: RCA ARL1-3522 CD: RCA/BMG 09026 612362

ROLAND HAYES

Roun' about de mountain, arranged by Paur

New York 7-18 December 1961	Orchestra and Chorus Paur	LP: Victor LM 2600/LSC 2600 CD: RCA/BMG 09026 881532

LEE HOIBY (Born 1926)

Always it's spring; There came a wind like a bugle; Wild nights

New York 26 January 1991	Garvey, piano	CD: RCA/BMG 09026 684352

FREDERICK HOLLANDER (1896-1976)

Falling in love again

Los Angeles 9-11 May 1967	Orchestra Previn	LP: Victor LM 2983/LSC 2983/ARL1-1029

EDWARD HOPKINS (1818-1901)

We three kings of Orient are, arranged by Meyer

Vienna 3-5 June 1961	Wiener Singverein VPO Karajan	LP: Decca LXT 5657/SXL 2294/JB 38 LP: London 5644/OSA 25280 CD: Decca 421 1032/448 9982

ROSAMUND JOHNSON

Lift ev'ry voice and sing, arranged by Gerhardt

London 10-13 May 1982	Ambrosian Singers National PO Gerhardt	LP: RCA ARL1-4528 CD: RCA/BMG 09026 681532

JEROME KERN (1885-1945)

They didn't believe me

Los Angeles 9-11 May 1967	Previn, piano Manne Brown	LP: Victor LM 2983/LSC 2983/ARL1-1029

MRS JOSEPH KNAPP

Blessed assurance

New York 4-7 April 1966	St.Thomas Choir Self	LP: Victor LM 2918/LSC 2918 CD: RCA/BMG 09026 681532

ERICH WOLFGANG KORNGOLD (1897-1957)

Die tote Stadt, excerpt (Glück das mir verblieb)

Walthamstow 7-15 July 1977	New Philharmonia Santi	LP: RCA ARL1-2529 CD: RCA/BMG 09026 612362

WILLIAM LAWRENCE

Let us break bread together on our knees, arranged by Paur

New York 7-18 December 1961	Orchestra Paur	LP: Victor LM 2600/LSC 2600 CD: RCA/BMG 09026 681532

RUGGIERO LEONCAVALLO (1858-1919)

I pagliacci, excerpt (Qual fiamma avea nel guardo)

Walthamstow 1-8 August 1979	Philharmonia H.Lewis	LP: RCA ARL1-3522 CD: RCA/BMG 09026 612362

FRANZ LISZT (1811-1886)

Oh quand je dors!; Comment disaient-ils?

Saint Paul 8 January 1985	Garvey, piano	LP: Pro Arte PAD 231 CD: Pro Arte CDD 231

ROBERT LOWRY (1826-1899)

I need thee every hour

New York 4-7 April 1966	St.Thomas Choir Self	LP: Victor LM 2918/LSC 2918 CD: RCA/BMG 681532

MARTIN LUTHER (1483-1546)

Ein' feste Burg ist unser Gott, arranged by Gerhardt

London 10-13 May 1982	Ambrosian Singers National PO Gerhardt	LP: RCA ARL1-4528 CD: RCA/BMG 09026 681532

ALBERT MALOTTE (1895-1964)

The Lord's prayer

New York 4-7 April 1966	St.Thomas Choir Self	LP: Victor LM 2918/LSC 2918 CD: RCA/BMG 09026 681522/09026 681532

JOSEPH MARX (1882-1964)

Marienlied; Waldseligkeit

New York 26 January 1991	Garvey, piano	CD: RCA/BMG 09026 884352

PIETRO MASCAGNI (1863-1945)

Cavalleria rusticana, excerpt (Voi lo sapete)

Walthamstow 7-15 July 1977	Bainbridge Philharmonia H.Lewis	LP: RCA ARL1-2529 CD: RCA/BMG 09026 612362

JULES MASSENET (1842-1912)

Manon, excerpt (Adieu notre petite table)

Rome 2-6 August 1965	RCA Italiana Orchestra Molinari-Pradelli	LP: Victor LM 2898/LSC 2898/ RB 6700/SB 6700 CD: RCA/BMG 09026 612362/09026 681532

Thais, excerpt (Dites-moi que je suis belle!)

Walthamstow 13-18 July 1969	LSO Downes	LP: Victor LSC 3163/SER 5589 CD: RCA/BMG 09026 612362

FELIX MENDELSSOHN-BARTHOLDY (1809-1847)

Hark the herald angels sing, arranged by Meyer

Vienna 3-5 June 1961	Wiener Singverein VPO Karajan	LP: Decca LXT 5657/SXL 2294/JB 38 LP: London 5644/OSA 25280 CD: Decca 421 1032/448 9982

GIAN CARLO MENOTTI (Born 1911)

Amelia al ballo, excerpt (While I waste these precious hours)

Walthamstow 7-15 July 1977	Philharmonia Santi	LP: RCA ARL1-2529 CD: RCA/BMG 09026 612362

GIACOMO MEYERBEER (1791-1864)

L'africaine, excerpt (Fils du soleil!)

Rome 2-6 August 1965	RCA Italiana Orchestra Molinari-Pradelli	LP: Victor LM 2898/LSC 2898/ RB 6700/SB 6700 CD: RCA/BMG 09026 612362
Munich 27 January 1968	Bavarian RO Franci	CD: Gala GL 328
Paris 15 February 1968	Orchestre National Rizchin	CD: Hunt CDGI 803

WOLFGANG AMADEUS MOZART (1756-1791)

Bella mia fiamma, concert aria

Walthamstow 4 June 1968	New Philharmonia Adler	LP: Victor LSC 3113/SB 6813 CD: RCA/BMG 09026 613572

Ch'io mi scordi di te?, concert aria

Walthamstow 3 June 1968	New Philharmonia Adler	LP: Victor LSC 3113/SB 6813 CD: RCA/BMG 09026 613572

Così fan tutte

New York 20 February 1965	<u>Role of Fiordiligi</u> Elias, Peters, Tucker, Uppmann, Guarrera Metropolitan Opera Orchestra & Chorus Rosenstock	Unpublished Met broadcast
Walthamstow 24 August- 8 September 1967	Troyanos, Raskin, Shirley, Milnes, Flagello Ambrosian Singers New Philharmonia Leinsdorf	LP: Victor LM 6416/LSC 6416/ SER 5575-5578 CD: RCA/BMG GD 86677 <u>Excerpts</u> CD: RCA/BMG 09026 681532

Così fan tutte, excerpt (Come scoglio!)

San Francisco 23 January 1973	San Francisco SO Ozawa	CD: Gala GL 328

Così fan tutte, excerpt (Ah guarda sorella!)

New York 28 March 1982	Horne Metropolitan Opera Orchestra Levine	CD: RCA/BMG 09026 681522/09026 681523 <u>Also unpublished video recording</u>

Don Giovanni

Vienna 11-24 June 1959	<u>Role of Elvira</u> Nilsson, Ratti, Valletti, Siepi, Corena, Van Mill, Blankenburg Vienna Opera Chorus VPO Leinsdorf	LP: Victor LM 6410/LSC 6410/ RE 25028-25031/SER 4528-4531 LP: Decca D10 D4 CD: Decca 444 5942 <u>Excerpts</u> LP: Decca GRV 10 CD: Decca 421 8752/440 4022/440 6542
Salzburg August 1960	<u>Role of Anna</u> Schwarzkopf, Sciutti, Valletti, Wächter, Berry, Panerai, Zaccaria Vienna Opera Chorus VPO Karajan	LP: Historical Recording Enterprises HRE 247 LP: Movimento musica 03.001 CD: Movimento musica 013.6012 CD: Hunt CDKAR 225 CD: Curcio-Hunt OP 6 <u>Excerpts</u> CD: Melodram MEL 18003 CD: Memories HR 4396-4397
New York 19 January 1963	Amara, Hurley, Peerce, Siepi, Corena, Wiemann, Uppmann Metropolitan Opera Orchestra & Chorus Maazel	Unpublished Met broadcast
Vienna 22 June 1963	Güden, Sciutti, Wunderlich, Wächter, Berry, Kreppel Vienna Opera Chorus VPO Karajan	CD: Verona 27065-27067
New York 13 April 1974	Zylis-Gara, Stratas, Burrows, Milnes, Berry, Morris, Michalski Metropolitan Opera Orchestra & Chorus Levine	Unpublished Met broadcast

Don Giovanni, excerpt (Or sai chi l'onore)

Rome 24-28 June 1967	De Palma RCA Italiana Orchestra Molinari-Pradelli	LP: Victor LM 2968/LSC 2968/SB 6742 CD: RCA/BMG 09026 612362/09026 613572/ 09026 681532

Don Giovanni, excerpt (Non mi dir)

Walthamstow 14 July 1969	LSO Downes	LP: Victor LSC 3163/SER 5589 LP: Metropolitan Opera MET 104 CD: RCA/BMG 09026 612362/09026 613572/ 09026 681532

Exsultate jubilate, Alleluia

Vienna 3-5 June 1961	VPO Karajan	45: Decca CEP 729/SEC 5112 LP: Decca LXT 5657/SXL 2294/JB 38/GRV 10 LP: London 5644/OSA 25280 CD: 421 1032/425 0162/436 4022/ 440 4022/440 6542/443 7622/ 448 9932

Idomeneo, excerpt (Se il padre perdei)

Walthamstow 6 June 1969	New Philharmonia Adler	LP: Victor LSC 3113/SB 6813 CD: RCA/BMG 09026 613572

Idomeneo, excerpt (D'Oreste d'Ajace!)

Walthamstow 7 July 1977	New Philharmonia Santi	LP: RCA ARL1-2529 CD: RCA/BMG 09026 612362/09026 613572
New York 26 January 1991	Garvey, piano	CD: RCA/BMG 09026 684352

Le nozze di Figaro, excerpt (Porgi amor)

Walthamstow 5 June 1968	New Philharmonia Adler	LP: Victor LSC 3113/SB 6813 CD: RCA/BMG 09026 613572

Le nozze di Figaro, excerpt (Dove sono)

Rome 2-6 August 1965	RCA Italiana Orchestra Molinari-Pradelli	LP: Victor LM 2898/LSC 2898/ RB 6700/SB 6700 CD: RCA/BMG 09026 612362/09026 613572/ 09026 681532
Munich 27 January 1968	Bavarian RO Franci	CD: Gala GL 328
Paris 15 February 1968	Orchestre National Rizchin	CD: Hunt CDGI 803
New York 22 April 1972	Metropolitan Opera Orchestra Molinari-Pradelli	LP: DG 2530 260 Also unpublished video recording
New York 28 March 1982	Metropolitan Opera Orchestra Levine	Unpublished Met broadcast and unpublished video recording

Le nozze di Figaro, excerpt (Deh vieni non tardar)

Walthamstow 6 June 1968	New Philharmonia Adler	LP: Victor LSC 3113/SB 6813 CD: RCA/BMG 09026 613572

Il re pastore, excerpt (L'amerò sarò costante)

Walthamstow 5 June 1968	New Philharmonia Adler	LP: Victor LSC 3113/SB 6813 CD: RCA/BMG 09026 613572

Requiem

Salzburg 24 August 1960	Rössel-Majdan, Wunderlich, Berry Wiener Singverein VPO Karajan	LP: Historical Recording Enterprises HRE 317 LP: Movimento musica 01.023 CD: Foyer CDS 16001 CD: Claque GM 2003-2004 CD: Priceless D 16573 CD issue on Melodram MEL 18003 purporting to contain this performance actually has a different Karajan version of the work without Leontyne Price

Die Zauberflöte, excerpt (Ach ich fühl's)

Walthamstow 5 June 1968	New Philharmonia Adler	LP: Victor LSC 3113/SB 6813 LP: Metropolitan Opera MET 104 CD: RCA/BMG 09026 613572

JACQUES OFFENBACH (1819-1880)

La périchole, excerpt (Tu n'es pas beau)

Walthamstow 14 July 1969	LSO Downes	LP: Victor LSC 3163/SER 5589 CD: RCA/BMG 09026 612362

FRANCIS POULENC (1899-1963)

Les dialogues des Carmélites, excerpt (Mes filles voilà que s'achève)

Walthamstow 14 July 1969	LSO Downes	LP: Victor LSC 3163/SER 5589 CD: RCA/BMG 09026 612362/09026 681532

Bleuet

New York 26 January 1991	Garvey, piano	CD: RCA/BMG 09026 684352

C'est ainsi que tu es

Saint Paul 8 January 1985	Garvey, piano	LP: Pro Arte PAD 231 CD: Pro Arte CDD 231

Main dominée par le coeur; Je nommerai ton front; Tu vois le feu du soir; Ce doux petit visage

New York 11 April 1958-9 January 1959	Garvey, piano	LP: Victor LM 2279/LSC 2279 CD: RCA/BMG 09026 614992/09026 681532

ANDRE PREVIN (Born 1929)

It's good to have you near again

Los Angeles 9-11 May 1967	Previn, piano	LP: Victor LM 2983/LSC 2983/ARL1-1029

Where, I wonder

Los Angeles 9-11 May 1967	Orchestra Previn	LP: Victor LM 2983/LSC 2983/ARL1-1029

FLORENCE PRICE (1888-1953)

My soul's been anchored in the Lord

New York 7-18 December 1961	Orchestra Paur	LP: Victor LM 2600/LSC 2600 CD: RCA/BMG 09026 681532 Arrangement by Paur
Saint Paul 8 January 1985	Garvey, piano	LP: Pro Arte PAD 231 CD: Pro Arte CDD 231

GIACOMO PUCCINI (1858-1924)

La Bohème, excerpt (Sì mi chiamano Mimì)

Walthamstow 20-25 July 1971	New Philharmonia Downes	LP: Victor LSC 3337/SER 5674 CD: RCA/BMG RD 85999

La Bohème, excerpt (Donde lieta uscì)

Walthamstow 20-25 July 1971	New Philharmonia Downes	LP: Victor LSC 3337/SER 5674 CD: RCA/BMG RD 85999/09026 681532

La Bohème, excerpt (Quando m'en vo)

Walthamstow 20-25 July 1971	New Philharmonia Downes	LP: Victor LSC 3337/SER 5674 CD: RCA/BMG RD 85999

Edgar, excerpt (Addio mio dolce amor!)

Walthamstow 20-25 July 1971	New Philharmonia Downes	LP: Victor LSC 3337/SER 5674 CD: RCA/BMG RD 85999

La fanciulla del West, excerpt (Laggiù nel Soledad)

Walthamstow 20-25 July 1971	New Philharmonia Downes	LP: Victor LSC 3337/SER 5674 CD: RCA/BMG RD 85999

Gianni Schicchi, excerpt (O mio babbino caro)

Walthamstow 13-18 July 1969	LSO Downes	LP: Victor LSC 3163/SER 5589 CD: RCA/BMG RD 85999/09026 612362

Madama Butterfly

Rome 10-20 July 1962	Role of Butterfly Elias, Tucker, Maero RCA Italiana Orchestra & Chorus Leinsdorf	LP: Victor LM 6160/LSC 6160/LMDS 6160/ RE 5504-5506/SER 5504-5506/ EK 26.35110 CD: RCA/BMG RD 86160/74321 394972 Excerpts LP: Victor LM 2840/LSC 2840/RB 6505/ RB 6542/RB 6680/SB 6505/SB 6542/ SB 6680 CD: RCA/BMG 09026 681532

Madama Butterfly, excerpt (Bimba non piangere!)

Walthamstow 21-25 July 1974	Bainbridge, Domingo New Philharmonia Santi	LP: RCA ARL1-0840/ARD1-0840 CD: RCA/BMG RD 85999

Madama Butterfly, excerpt (Un bel dì)

Rome 27-29 June 1960	Rome Opera Orchestra De Fabritiis	LP: Victor LM 2506/LSC 2506/ RB 6505/SB 6505 CD: RCA/BMG 09026 681522/09026 681532
Walthamstow 20-25 July 1971	New Philharmonia Downes	LP: Victor LSC 3337/SER 5674 LP: Metropolitan Opera MET 104 CD: RCA/BMG RD 85999
New York 26 January 1991	Garvey, piano	CD: RCA/BMG 09026 684352

Madama Butterfly, excerpt (Scuoti quella fronda!)

New York 28 March 1982	Horne Metropolitan Opera Orchestra Levine	CD: RCA/BMG 09026 681532 Also unpublished video recording

Madama Butterfly, excerpt (Tu piccolo iddio!)

Rome 27-29 June 1960	Rome Opera Orchestra De Fabritiis	LP: Victor LM 2506/LSC 2506/ RB 6505/SB 6505 CD: RCA/BMG 09026 681532
New York 26 January 1991	Garvey, piano	CD: RCA/BMG 09026 684352

Manon Lescaut, excerpt (In quelle trine morbide)

Walthamstow 20-25 July 1971	New Philharmonia Downes	LP: Victor LSC 3337/SER 5674 LP: Metropolitan Opera MET 104 CD: RCA/BMG 09026 681532/RD 85999

Manon Lescaut, excerpt (Sola perduta abbandonata)

Walthamstow 20-25 July 1971	New Philharmonia Downes	LP: Victor LSC 3337/SER 5674 CD: RCA/BMG RD 85999/09026 681532

Manon Lescaut, excerpt (Tu tu amore!)

Walthamstow 21-25 July 1974	Domingo New Philharmonia Santi	LP: RCA ARL1-0840/ARD1-0840 CD: RCA/BMG 09026 616342/09026 681532

La rondine, excerpt (Ore dolci e divine)

Walthamstow 20-25 July 1971	New Philharmonia Downes	LP: Victor LSC 3337/SER 5674 CD: RCA/BMG RD 85999/09026 681522/ 09026 681532

La rondine, excerpt (Chi il bel sogno di Doretta)

Rome 27-29 June 1960	Rome Opera Orchestra De Fabritiis	LP: Victor LM 2506/LSC 2506 RB 6505/SB 6505 CD: RCA/BMG 09026 681532
Munich 27 January 1968	Bavarian RO Franci	CD: Gala GL 328
Paris 15 February 1968	Orchestre National Rizchin	CD: Hunt CDGI 803
New York 28 March 1982	Metropolitan Opera Orchestra Levine	Unpublished Met broadcast and unpublished video recording
New York 26 January 1991	Garvey, piano	CD: RCA/BMG 09026 684352

Suor Angelica, excerpt (Senza mamma)

Rome 24-28 June 1967	RCA Italiana Orchestra Molinari-Pradelli	LP: Victor LM 2968/LSC 2968/SB 6742 CD: RCA/BMG 09026 612362/09026 681532
Munich 27 January 1968	Bavarian RO Franci	CD: Gala GL 328
Paris 15 February 1968	Orchestre National Rizchin	CD: Hunt CDGI 803

Il tabarro

Walthamstow 28 June- 2 July 1971	Role of Giorgetta Dominguez, Domingo, Milnes Alldis Choir New Philharmonia Leinsdorf	LP: Victor LSC 3220/SER 5619/AW26.41112 CD: RCA/BMG GD 60865

Tosca

New York 7 April 1962	Role of Tosca Corelli, MacNeil Metropolitan Opera Orchestra & Chorus Adler	LP: Teatro dischi TD 101 CD: Myto MCD 92570 Excerpts LP: Historical Recording Enterprises HRE 287 These excerpts are incorrectly described as conducted by Karajan in Vienna November 1963
Vienna 16-30 September 1962	Di Stefano, Taddei Vienna Opera Chorus VPO Karajan	LP: Victor LD 7022/LDS 7022/ RE 5507-5508/SER 5507-5508/ LP: Decca 5BB 123-124/EK 635.232 LP: London OSA 1284 CD: Decca 421 6702/452 6202 Excerpts LP: Victor RB 6655/SB 6655 LP: Decca GRV 10 CD: Decca 440 4022/440 6542/452 7282
Walthamstow 31 July- 11 August 1972	Domingo, Milnes Alldis Choir New Philharmonia Mehta	LP: RCA ARL2-0105/EX 26.35062 CD: RCA/BMG RD 80105/74321 395032 Excerpts LP: RCA RL 10567 LP: Metropolitan Opera MET 104 CD: RCA/BMG 09026 616342

Tosca, excerpt (Vissi d'arte)

Rome 27-29 June 1960	Rome Opera Orchestra De Fabritiis	LP: Victor LM 2506/LSC 2506/ RB 6505/SB 6505 CD: RCA/BMG 09026 681532
Paris 15 February 1968	Orchestre National Rizchin	CD: Hunt CDGI 803
Walthamstoq 20-25 July 1971	New Philharmonia Downes	LP: Victor LSC 3337/SER 5674 CD: RCA/BMG RD 85999
San Francisco 23 January 1973	San Francisco SO Ozawa	CD: Gala GL 328
Saint Paul 8 January 1985	Garvey, piano	LP: Pro Arte PAD 231 CD: Pro Arte CDD 231
New York 26 January 1991	Garvey, piano	CD: RCA/BMG 09026 684352

Turandot

Vienna June 1961	Role of Liù Nilsson, Di Stefano, Zaccaria Vienna Opera Chorus VPO Molinari-Pradelli	LP: Morgan MOR 6101 LP: Historical Recording Enterprises HRE 231 CD: Legato LCD 153 Excerpts CD: Memories HR 4396-4397

Turandot, excerpt (In questa reggia)

Walthamstow 7-15 July 1977	Barioni Ambrosian Singers New Philharmonia Santi	LP: RCA ARL1-2529 CD: RCA/BMG RD 85999/09026 612362

Turandot, excerpt (Signore ascolta)

Rome 27-29 June 1960	Rome Opera Orchestra De Fabritiis	LP: Victor LM 2506/LSC 2506/ RB 6505/SB 6505 LP: Metropolitan Opera MET 104 CD: RCA/BMG 09026 681532

Turandot, excerpt (Tu che di gel sei cinta)

Rome 27-29 June 1960	Rome Opera Orchestra De Fabritiis	LP: Victor LM 2506/LSC 2506/ RB 6505/SB 6505 CD: RCA/BMG 09026 681532

Le villi, excerpt (Se come voi piccina io fossi)

Walthamstow 20-25 July 1971	New Philharmonia Downes	LP: Victor LSC 3337/SER 5674 CD: RCA/BMG RD 85999

HENRY PURCELL (1659-1695)

Dido and Aeneas, excerpt (When I am laid in earth)

Rome 2-6 August 1965	RCA Italiana Orchestra Molinari-Pradelli	LP: Victor LM 2898/LSC 2898/ RB 6700/SB 6700 CD: RCA/BMG 09026 612362/09026 681532

RICHARD RODGERS (1902-1979)

Climb every mountain

New York 16 March 1971	Swann, organ	LP: Victor LM 3219

Hello young lovers; It never entered my mind; Nobody's heart

Los Angeles 9-11 May 1967	Orchestra Previn	LP: Victor LM 2983/LSC 2983/ARL1-1029

GIOACHINO ROSSINI (1792-1868)

Duetto buffo di 2 gatti

1982	Crespin	LP: Legendary LR 200

FRANZ SCHUBERT (1797-1828)

Ave Maria, arranged by Sabatini

Vienna 3-5 June 1961	VPO Karajan	45: Decca CEP 729/SEC 5112 LP: Decca LXT 5657/SXL 2294/JB 38/GRV 10 LP: London 5644/OSA 25280 CD: Decca 421 1032/440 4022/440 6542/ 444 5462/448 9982/452 2082
New York 4-7 April 1966	St.Thomas Choir Self	LP: Victor LM 2918/LSC 2918 CD: RCA/BMG 09026 681532

Lieder: Die junge Nonne; Nacht und Träume; Liebesbotschaft; Ave Maria; Gretchen am Spinnrade; So lasst mich scheinen; Die Allmacht

New York 7 March- 16 May 1979	Garvey, piano	LP: Angel 37631

ROBERT SCHUMANN (1810-1856)

Frauenliebe und -Leben, song cycle

New York 30 April- 19 May 1969	Garvey, piano	LP: Victor LSC 3169/SER 5594 CD: RCA/BMG 09026 681532

Lieder: Schöne Wiege meiner Leiden; Er ist's!; Heiss mich nicht reden; Lust der Sturmnacht; Widmung; Mignon

New York 30 April- 19 May 1969	Garvey, piano	LP: Victor LSC 3169/SER 5594 CD: RCA/BMG 09026 681532

JOHANN STRAUSS (1825-1899)

Die Fledermaus, excerpt (Klänge der Heimat)

Walthamstow 7-15 July 1977	New Philharmonia Santi	LP: RCA ARL1-2529 CD: RCA/BMG 09026 612362

SALZBURGER FESTSPIELE 1960

40 JAHRE SALZBURGER FESTSPIELE

DON GIOVANNI

DRAMMA GIOCOSO IN ZWEI AKTEN
VON LORENZO DA PONTE

MUSIK VON
WOLFGANG AMADEUS MOZART

DIRIGENT
HERBERT VON KARAJAN

INSZENIERUNG
OSCAR FRITZ SCHUH

BÜHNENBILD
TEO OTTO

KOSTÜME
GEORGE WAKHEWITCH

ORCHESTER
DIE WIENER PHILHARMONIKER
CHOR DER WIENER STAATSOPER

DON GIOVANNI

(in italienischer Sprache)

Dramma giocoso in zwei Akten von Lorenzo da Ponte

MUSIK VON WOLFGANG AMADEUS MOZART

Don Giovanni	Eberhard Wächter
Donna Elvira	Elisabeth Schwarzkopf
Il Commendatore . . .	Nicola Zaccaria
Donna Anna	Leontyne Price
Don Ottavio	Cesare Valletti
Leporello	Walter Berry
Zerline	Graziella Sciutti
Masetto	Rolando Panerai

Technische Einrichtung und Beleuchtung: Sepp Nordegg

Nach dem ersten Aufzug eine größere Pause

RICHARD STRAUSS (1864-1949)

Die ägyptische Helena, excerpt (Zweite Brautnacht!)

Boston 22-24 April 1965	Boston SO Leinsdorf	LP: Victor LM 2849/LSC 2849/ RB 6639/SB 6639 CD: RCA/BMG GD 60398/09026 681532
Munich 27 January 1968	Bavarian RO Franci	CD: Gala GL 328

Ariadne auf Naxos

London 27 November- 6 December 1977	<u>Role of Ariadne/</u> <u>Primadonna</u> Gruberova, Troyanos, Kollo, Berry, Kunz LPO Solti	LP: Decca D103 D3/GF 635.458 LP: London OSAD 13131 CD: Decca 430 3842 <u>Excerpts</u> LP: Decca GRV 10 CD: Decca 440 4022/440 6542

Ariadne auf Naxos, excerpt (Es gibt ein Reich)

Walthamstow 9-23 July 1970	LSO Cleva	LP: Victor LM 3218/LSC 3218/SER 5621 CD: RCA/BMG GD 60398/09026 681532

Die Frau ohne Schatten, excerpt (Sieh Amme, sieh des Mannes Aug'!)

Walthamstow 9-11 July 1973	P.Clark Ambrosian Singers New Philharmonia Leinsdorf	LP: RCA ARL1-0333/TRL1-7044/CML 082 CD: RCA/BMG GD 60398/GD 86722/ 09026 681532

Guntram, excerpt (Fass' ich sie bang)

Walthamstow 9-11 July 1973	New Philharmonia Leinsdorf	LP: RCA ARL1-0333 CD: RCA/BMG 60398

Der Rosenkavalier, excerpt (Da geht er hin)

Walthamstow 9-11 July 1973	New Philharmonia Leinsdorf	LP: RCA ARL1-0333/TRL1-7044 CD: RCA/BMG GD 60398

Salome, excerpt (Du wolltest mich nicht deinen Mund küssen lassen)

Boston 22-24 April 1965	Boston SO Leinsdorf	LP: Victor LM 2849/LSC 2849/ RB 6639/SB 6639 CD: RCA/BMG GD 60398/09026 681532

4 letzte Lieder

Walthamstow 6-7 July 1973	New Philharmonia Leinsdorf	LP: RCA AR11-0333/CML 082 CD: RCA/BMG GD 86722/09026 681532 Beim Schlafengehen CD: RCA/BMG 09026 681522

Allerseelen

New York 9 April 1958-9 January 1959	Garvey, piano	LP: Victor LM 2279/LSC 2279 CD: RCA/BMG 09026 614992/09026 681532

Als mir dein Lied erklang

New York 7 March-16 May 1979	Garvey, piano	LP: Angel 37631

Befreit

New York 7 March-16 May 1979	Garvey, piano	LP: Angel 37631
New York 26 January 1991	Garvey, piano	CD: RCA/BMG 09026 684352

Breit über mein Haupt

New York 7 March-16 May 1979	Garvey, piano	LP: Angel 37631

Cäcilie

New York 7 March-16 May 1979	Garvey, piano	LP: Angel 37631

Freundliche Vision

New York 9 April 1958-9 January 1959	Garvey, piano	LP: Victor LM 2279/LSC 2279 CD: RCA/BMG 09026 614992/09026 681532

Heimkehr

New York 7 March-16 May 1979	Garvey, piano	LP: Angel 37631

Herr Lenz

New York 26 January 1991	Garvey, piano	CD: RCA/BMG 09026 684352

Ich liebe dich

Saint Paul 8 January 1985	Garvey, piano	LP: Pro Arte PAD 231 CD: Pro Arte CDD 231
New York 26 January 1991	Garvey, piano	CD: RCA/BMG 09026 684352

Morgen

New York 7 March- 16 May 1979	Garvey, piano	LP: Angel 37631

Die Nacht

Saint Paul 8 January 1985	Garvey, piano	LP: Pro Arte PAD 231 CD: Pro Arte CDD 231

Schlagende Herzen

New York 9 April 1958- 9 January 1959	Garvey, piano	LP: Victor LM 2279/LSC 2279 CD: RCA/BMG 09026 614992/09026 681532

Seitdem dein Aug'

New York 7 March- 16 May 1979	Garvey, piano	LP: Angel 37631

Ständchen

Saint Paul 8 January 1985	Garvey, piano	LP: Pro Arte PAD 231 CD: Pro Arte CDD 231

Der Stern

Saint Paul 8 January 1985	Garvey, piano	LP: Pro Arte PAD 231 CD: Pro Arte CDD 231

Wasserrose

New York 7 March- 16 May 1979	Garvey, piano	LP: Angel 37631

Wie sollten wir geheim sie halten

New York 9 April 1958- 9 January 1959	Garvey, piano	LP: Victor LM 2279/LSC 2279 CD: RCA/BMG 09026 614992/09026 681532

Zueignung

Saint Paul 8 January 1985	Garvey, piano	LP: Pro Arte PAD 231 CD: Pro Arte CDD 231

BILLY TAYLOR

I wish I knew how it would feel to be free, arranged by Bonds

New York 19-22 April 1970	Rust College Choir Holmes	LP: Victor LM 3183/LSC 3183 CD: RCA/BMG 09026 681532

PIOTR TCHAIKOVSKY (1840-1893)

Evgeny Onegin, excerpt (Tatiana's letter scene)

Walthamstow 9-23 July 1970	LSO Cleva	LP: Victor LM 3218/LSC 3218/ SER 5621/TRL1-7044 CD: RCA/BMG 09026 681532

GIUSEPPE VERDI (1813-1901)

Requiem

Vienna 28 May- 26 June 1960	Elias, Björling, Tozzi Wiener Singverein VPO Reiner	LP: Victor LD 6091/LDS 6091/ RE 25026-25027/SER 4526-4527 LP: Decca DJB 2003 LP: London OSA 1294/JB 42004 CD: Decca 421 6082/444 8332 <u>Excerpts</u> LP: Decca GRV 10 CD: Decca 440 4022/440 6542
New York 28 March 1964	Elias, Bergonzi, Siepi Metropolitan Opera Orchestra & Chorus Solti	Unpublished Met broadcast
Moscow 25 September 1964	Cossotto, Bergonzi, Zaccaria La Scala Orchestra & Chorus Karajan	LP: Melodiya M10 457 85005 LP: Foyer FO 1045 CD: Foyer 2CF-2012
Milan 16 January 1967	Cossotto, Pavarotti, Ghiaurov La Scala Orchestra & Chorus Karajan	CD: Butterfly BMCD 013 CD: Frequenz 043.510 VHS Video: DG 072 1423 Laserdisc: DG 072 1421 <u>Excerpts</u> CD: Memories HR 4396-4397
Chicago 1-2 June 1977	Baker, Luchetti, Van Dam Chicago SO and Chorus Solti	LP: RCA RL 02476/ARL2-2476 CD: RCA/BMG RD 82476/09026 614032 <u>Excerpts</u> CD: RCA/BMG 09026 681532
New York 20 February 1982	Quivar, Domingo, Cheek Metropolitan Opera Orchestra & Chorus Levine	Unpublished Met broadcast

Aida

Rome 24 June- 26 July 1961	Role of Aida Gorr, Vickers, Merrill, Tozzi, Clabassi Rome Opera Orchestra & Chorus Solti	LP: Victor LM 6158/LSC 6158/ RE 25038-25040/SER 4538-4540 LP: Decca SET 427-429 LP: London OSA 1393 CD: Decca 417 4162 Excerpts LP: Victor LM 2616/LSC 2616 LP: Decca JB 81/GRV 10 CD: Decca 421 8602/440 4022/440 6542
Vienna 1963	Simionato, Usunow, Bastianini Vienna Opera Chorus VPO Matacic	LP: Foyer FO 1036 Excerpts CD: Memories HR 4396-4397
New York 7 December 1963	Gorr, Bergonzi, Sereni, Siepi Metropolitan Opera Orchestra & Chorus Solti	Unpublished Met broadcast
New York 12 February 1966	Dalis, Tucker, Merrill, Ghiuselev Metropolitan Opera Orchestra & Chorus Mehta	Unpublished Met broadcast
New York 13 March 1966	Cernei, Corelli, Milnes, Hines Metropolitan Opera Orchestra & Chorus Mehta	CD: Great Operatic Performances GOP 733
New York 25 February 1967	Bumbry, Bergonzi, Merrill, Hines Metropolitan Opera Orchestra & Chorus Schippers	Unpublished Met broadcast

In the presence of His Royal Highness The Prince of Wales

VERDI REQUIEM

SIR GEORG SOLTI

Leontyne Price

Yvonne Minton

Veriano Luchetti

Martti Talvela

London Philharmonic Orchestra
Leader: DAVID NOLAN

London Philharmonic Choir
Conductor: JOHN ALLDIS

Philharmonia Chorus
Chorus Master: NORBERT BALATSCH

This concert is being broadcast by BBC Radio 3

ROYAL ALBERT HALL
General Manager: ANTHONY J. CHARLTON

SUNDAY 16 DECEMBER 1979 at 7.30

SALZBURGER FESTSPIELE 1962

DRITTES ORCHESTERKONZERT

GIUSEPPE VERDI

REQUIEM

Dirigent
HERBERT VON KARAJAN

Solisten:
LEONTYNE PRICE
GIULIETTA SIMIONATO
GIUSEPPE ZAMPIERI
NICOLAI GJAUROFF

DAS BERLINER PHILHARMONISCHE ORCHESTER
DER SINGVEREIN DER GESELLSCHAFT DER MUSIKFREUNDE WIEN

Aida/concluded

New York 3 January 1970	Dalis, J.Thomas, Merrill, Macurdy Metropolitan Opera Orchestra & Chorus Molinari-Pradelli	Unpublished Met broadcast
Walthamstow 9-23 July 1970	Bumbry, Domingo, Milnes, Raimondi Alldis Choir LSO Leinsdorf	LP: Victor LSC 6198/LMDS 6198/ SER 5609-5611 CD: RCA/BMG RD 86198/74321 394982 Excerpts LP: Victor LSC 3275/RL 42090 LP: Metropolitan Opera MET 104 CD: RCA/BMG 09026 616342/09026 681532
New York 6 March 1976	Horne, Domingo, MacNeil, Giaiotti Metropolitan Opera Orchestra & Chorus Levine	Unpublished Met broadcast
New York 3 January 1985	Cossotto, McCracken, Estes, Macurdy, Kavrakos Metropolitan Opera Orchestra & Chorus Levine	Unpublished Met broadcast

Aida, Act 3

New York 10 February 1973	Kraft, Tagliavini, MacNeil, Morris Metropolitan Opera Orchestra Molinari-Pradelli	CD: Great Operatic Performances GOP 736 Gala performance

Aida, excerpt (Ritorna vincitor)

Rome 27-29 June 1960	Rome Opera Orchestra De Fabritiis	LP: Victor LM 2506/LSC 2506/RB 6505/ SB 6505/VCS 7063/DPS 2001

Aida, excerpt (O patria mia)

Rome 27-29 June 1960	Rome Opera Orchestra De Fabritiis	LP: Victor LM 2506/LSC 2506/RB 6505/ SB 6505/VCS 7063/DPS 2001

Aida, excerpt (Fu la sorte)

New York 28 March 1982	Horne Metropolitan Opera Orchestra Levine	CD: RCA/BMG 09026 681532 Also unpublished video recording

Un ballo in maschera

New York 26 February 1966	Role of Amelia Dunn, Peters, Merrill, Macurdy Metropolitan Opera Orchestra & Chorus Molinari-Pradelli	Unpublished Met broadcast
Rome 8-21 June 1966	Verrett, Grist, Bergonzi, Merrill, Flagello RCA Italiana Orchestra & Chorus Leinsdorf	LP: Victor LM 6179/LSC 6179/LMDS 6179/ RE 5556-5558/SER 5710-5712/ EX 26.35123 CD: RCA/BMG GD 86645 Excerpts LP: Victor LM 3034/LSC 3034/ VCS 7063/DPS 2001 LP: Metropolitan Opera MET 104 CD: RCA/BMG RCD 17016/09026 681532
New York 6 April 1968	Rankin, Peters, Prevedi, Merrill, Avary Metropolitan Opera Orchestra & Chorus Schippers	Unpublished Met broadcast

Un ballo in maschera, excerpt (Teco io sto!)

Walthamstow 21-25 July 1974	Domingo New Philharmonia Santi	LP: RCA ARL1-0840/ARD1-0840 CD: RCA/BMG 09026 616342
New York 22 October 1983	Pavarotti Metropolitan Opera Orchestra Levine	Unpublished radio broadcast and unpublished video recording Performed at Met centennial gala

Don Carlo, excerpt (Tu che la vanità)

	LSO Cleva	LP: Victor LM 3218/LSC 3218/ SER 5621/TRL1-7044 CD: RCA/BMG 09026 681532
San Francisco 23 January 1973	San Francisco SO Ozawa	CD: Gala GL 328

Ernani

	Role of Elvira	
New York 10 April 1965	Corelli, Sereni, Siepi Metropolitan Opera Orchestra & Chorus Schippers	LP: Great Operatic Performances GOP 10 CD: Great Operatic Performances GOP 702 CD: Memories HR 4370-4371 CD: Verona 27025-27026
New York 1 December 1965	Bergonzi, MacNeil, Tozzi Metropolitan Opera Orchestra & Chorus Schippers	LP: Movimento musica 03.020 CD: Movimento musica Excerpts CD: Memories HR 4396-4397 CD: Legato LCD 161
Rome 3-20 July 1967	Bergonzi, Sereni, Flagello RCA Italiana Orchestra & Chorus Schippers	LP: Victor LM 6183/LSC 6183/LMDS 6183/ RE 5572-5574/SER 5572-5574/ GF 26.35024 CD: RCA/BMG GD 86503 Excerpts LP: Victor LM 3035/LSC 3035/ VCS 7063/DPS 2001 CD: RCA/BMG 09026 681532/RCD 17016

Ernani, excerpt (Ernani involami!)

Munich 27 January 1968	Bavarian RO Franci	CD: Gala GL 328
Paris 15 February 1968	Orchestre National Rizchin	CD: Hunt CDGI 803

La forza del destino

Rome 20 July- 5 August 1964	<u>Role of Leonora</u> Verrett, Tucker, Merrill, Tozzi RCA Italiana Orchestra & Chorus Schippers	LP: Victor LM 6413/LSC 6413/LMDS 6413 RE 5527-5530/SER 5527-5530 CD: RCA/BMG GD 87971 <u>Excerpts</u> LP: Victor LM 2838/LSC 2838/RB 6679/ SB 6679/VCS 7063/DPS 2001 CD: RCA/BMG 09026 681522/09026 681532
New York 9 March 1968	Pearl, Corelli, Merrill, Corena Metropolitan Opera Orchestra & Chorus Molinari-Pradelli	CD: Myto MCD 945112
New York 12 February 1972	Casei, Bergonzi, Paskalis, Siepi Metropolitan Opera Orchestra & Chorus Veltri	Unpublished Met broadcast
Walthamstow 31 July- 10 August 1976	Cossotto, Domingo, Milnes, Giaiotti Alldis Choir LSO Levine	LP: RCA RL 01864/ARL4-1864 CD: RCA/BMG RD 81864/74321 395022
New York 12 March 1977	Elias, Domingo, MacNeil, Talvela Metropolitan Opera Orchestra & Chorus Levine	Unpublished Met broadcast
New York 24 March 1984	I.Jones, Giacomini, Nucci, Giaiotti Metropolitan Opera Orchestra & Chorus Levine	VHS Video: DG 072 4271 Laserdisc: DG 072 4273

La forza del destino, excerpt (Pace pace mio dio!)

New York 1 January 1967	Bell Telephone Orchestra Voshees	CD: Great Operatic Performances GOP 736
New York 28 March 1982	Metropolitan Opera Orchestra Levine	Unpublished video recording and unpublished radio broadcast
Saint Paul 8 January 1985	Garvey, piano	LP: Pro Arte PAD 231 CD: Pro Arte CDD 231
New York 26 January 1991	Garvey, piano	CD: RCA/BMG 09026 684352

I Lombardi, excerpt (Se vano e il pregare)

Walthamstow 14 July 1969	LSO Downes	LP: Victor LSC 3163/SER 5589 CD: RCA/BMG 09026 612362

Macbeth, excerpt (La luce langue)

Walthamstow 7-15 July 1977	New Philharmonia Santi	LP: RCA ARL1-2529 CD: RCA/BMG 09026 612362

Macbeth, excerpt (Una macchia è qui tuttora)

Rome 24-28 June 1967	Vozza, El Hage RCA Italiana Orchestra Molinari-Pradelli	LP: Victor LM 2968/LSC 2968/SB 6742/ VCS 7063/DPS 2001 CD: RCA/BMG RCD 17016/09026 612362/ 09026 681532

Otello, excerpt (Piangea cantando/Ave Maria)

Rome 2-6 August 1965	Vozza RCA Italiana Orchestra Molinari-Pradelli	LP: Victor LM 2898/LSC 2898/RB 6700/ SB 6700/VCS 7063/DPS 2001 CD: RCA/BMG RCD 17016/09026 612362/ 09026 681532

Otello, excerpt (Già nella notte)

Walthamstow 21-25 July 1974	Domingo New Philharmonia Santi	LP: RCA ARL1-0840/ARD1-0840 CD: RCA/BMG 09026 616342/ 09026 681522/09026 681532

Rigoletto, excerpt (Caro nome)

Walthamstow 1-8 August 1979	Philharmonia H.Lewis	LP: RCA ARL1-3522 CD: RCA/BMG 09026 612362

Simon Boccanegra, excerpt (Come in quest' ora)

Walthamstow 13-18 July 1969	LSO Downes	LP: Victor LSC 3163/SER 5589 CD: RCA/BMG 09026 612362

La traviata, excerpt (Ah fors è lui!/Sempre libera!)

Walthamstow 9-23 July 1970	R.Davies LSO Cleva	LP: Victor LM 3218/LSC 3218/ SER 5621/TRL1-7044 CD: RCA/BMG 09026 681532

La traviata, excerpt (Addio del passato)

Rome 2-6 August 1965	RCA Italiana Orchestra Molinari-Pradelli	LP: Victor LM 2898/LSC 2898/RB 6700/ SB 6700/VCS 7063/DPS 2001 CD: RCA RCD 17016/09026 612362

Il trovatore

Rome 15-24 July 1959	Role of Leonora Elias, Tucker, Warren, Tozzi Rome Opera Orchestra & Chorus Basile	LP: Victor LM 6150/LSC 6150/AGL3-4146 CD: RCA/BMG GD 60560 Excerpts LP: Victor LM 2506/LM 2617/LSC 2506/ LSC 2617/RB 6505/RB 6519/SB 6505/ SB 6519/VCS 7063/DPS 2001 CD: RCA/BMG 09026 681532 CD: Symphony SYCD 6164
New York 4 February 1961	Dalis, Corelli, Merrill, Wildermann Metropolitan Opera Orchestra & Chorus Cleva	CD: Myto MCD 91751
Salzburg 31 July 1962	Simionato, Corelli, Bastianini, Zaccaria Vienna Opera Chorus VPO Karajan	LP: Morgan MOR 6201 LP: Historical Recording Enterprises HRE 287 LP: Cetra ARK 7 LP: Movimento musica 03.018 LP: Melodram MEL 710 LP: Paragon DSV 52025 CD: Movimento musica 012.001 CD: Rodolphe RPC 32482-32483 CD: Hunt CDKAR 228 CD: Curcio-Hunt/Opera viva OP 8 CD: Priceless D 20791 CD: Gala GL 100.505 CD: DG 447 6592 Excerpts LP: Legendary LR 167 CD: Legato BIM 702 CD: Opera viva 1 CD: Hunt CDGI 803/Originals SH 962 CD: Memories HR 4396-4397/HR 4400-4401
New York 18 January 1964	Dalis, Tucker, Merrill, Macurdy Metropolitan Opera Orchestra & Chorus Schippers	Unpublished Met broadcast
New York 29 March 1969	Bumbry, McCracken, Milnes, Macurdy Metropolitan Opera Orchestra & Chorus Mehta	Unpublished Met broadcast

Il trovatore/concluded

Walthamstow 19-30 August 1969	Cossotto, Domingo, Milnes, Giaiotti Ambrosian Singers New Philharmonia Mehta	LP: Victor LSC 6194/LMDS 6194/ SER 5586-5588/GF 26.35025 CD: RCA/BMG RD 86194/74321 395042 Excerpts LP: Victor LSC 3203 LP: Metropolitan Opera MET 104 CD: RCA/BMG 09026 681522/09026 681532
Vienna May 1977	C.Ludwig, Pavarotti, Cappuccilli, Van Dam Vienna Opera Chorus VPO Karajan	CD: Artists' Live Recordings FED 002-003
Berlin September 1977	Obraztsova Bonisolli, Cappuccilli, Raimondi Deutsche Oper Chorus BPO Karajan	LP: EMI SLS 5111/EX 29 09533 LP: Angel 3855 CD: EMI CMS 769 3112
New York 6 February 1982	Cortez, Giacomini, Quilico, Cheek Metropolitan Opera Orchestra & Chorus Conlon	Unpublished Met broadcast

Il trovatore, excerpt (D'amor sull' ali rosee)

New York 16 April 1966	Metropolitan Opera Orchestra Cleva	LP: MRF Records MRF 7 Performed at gala farewell to old Metropolitan opera house

DER TROUBADOUR

(in italienischer Sprache)

Oper in vier Akten (acht Bildern)
nach einem Drama des Antonio Garcia Gutierrez von Salvatore Cammarano

MUSIK VON GIUSEPPE VERDI

Der Graf von Luna	Ettore Bastianini
Leonore	Leontyne Price
Azucena, Zigeunerin	Giulietta Simionato
Manrico	Franco Corelli
Ferrando	Nicola Zaccaria
Ines	Laurence Dutoit
Ruiz	Siegfried Rudolf Frese
Ein alter Zigeuner	Rudolf Zimmer
Ein Bote	Kurt Equiluz

Gefährtinnen Leonores, Nonnen, Krieger, Diener des Grafen,
Zigeuner und Zigeunerinnen

Ort der Handlung: Arragon und Biskaya zu Beginn des XV. Jahrhunderts

Einstudierung der Chöre: Roberto Benaglio

Technische Einrichtung und Beleuchtung: Sepp Nordegg

Pause nach dem vierten Bild

Großes Festspielhaus

GIUSEPPE VERDI

DER TROUBADOUR

Oper in vier Aufzügen (acht Bildern)

nach einem Drama des Antonio Garcia Gutierrez
von Salvatore Cammarano

Künstlerische Leitung
HERBERT VON KARAJAN

Bühnenbild: Teo Otto
Projektionen: Günther Schneider-Siemssen
Kostüme: Georges Wakhevitch

Der Graf von Luna	Piero Cappuccilli
Leonore	Leontyne Price
Azucena	Fiorenza Cossotto
Manrico	Franco Bonisolli
Ferrando	José van Dam
Ines	Maria Venuti
Ruiz	Heinz Zednik
Ein alter Zigeuner	Martin Egel
Ein Bote	Ewald Aichberger

Gefährtinnen Leonores, Nonnen, Anhänger des Grafen, Krieger, Zigeuner und Zigeunerinnen

Die Handlung spielt teils in Biscaya, teils in Aragonien zu Beginn des XV. Jahrhunderts

BERLINER PHILHARMONIKER
WIENER STAATSOPERNCHOR

Choreinstudierung: Walter Hagen-Groll
Technische Einrichtung und Beleuchtung: Helmuth Reichmann

RICHARD WAGNER (1813-1883)

Tannhäuser, excerpt (Dich teure Halle!)

Walthamstow 7-15 July 1977	New Philharmonia Santi	LP: RCA ARL1-2529 CD: RCA/BMG 09026 612362

Tristan und Isolde, excerpt (Mild und leise)

Walthamstow 1-8 August 1979	Philharmonia H.Lewis	LP: RCA ARL1-3522 CD: RCA/BMG 09026 612362

Die Walküre, excerpt (Du bist der Lenz)

Walthamstow 14 July 1969	LSO Downes	LP: Victor LM 3163/SER 5589 CD: RCA/BMG 09026 612362

JULIA WARD HOWE

Battle hymn of the Republic, arranged by Gerhardt

London 10-13 May 1982	Ambrosian Singers National PO Gerhardt	LP: RCA ARL1-4528 CD: RCA/BMG 09026 681532

SAMUEL WARD

America the beautiful

London 10-13 May 1982	Ambrosian Singers National PO Gerhardt	LP: RCA ARL1-4528 CD: RCA/BMG 09026 681532 Arrangement by Gerhardt
New York 26 January 1991	Garvey, piano	CD: RCA/BMG 09026 684352
New York 10 November 1991	Collegiate Chorale Orchestra Conlon	CD: RCA/BMG 09026 615092

CARL MARIA VON WEBER (1786-1826)

Der Freischütz, excerpt (Leise leise)

Rome 24-28 June 1967	RCA Italiana Orchestra Molinari-Pradelli	LP: Victor LM 2968/LSC 2968/SB 6742 CD: RCA/BMG 09026 612362

SAMUEL WESLEY (1766-1837)

The Church's one foundation

New York 4-7 April 1966	St.Thomas Choir Self	LP: Victor LM 2918/LSC 2918 CD: RCA/BMG 09026 681532

WILLIS

It came upon the midnight clear, arranged by Meyer

Vienna 3-5 June 1961	VPO Karajan	LP: Decca LXT 5657/SXL 2294/JB 38 LP: London 5644/OSA 25280 CD: Decca 421 1032/448 9982

HUGO WOLF (1860-1903)

Lieder: Der Gärtner; Lebewohl; Morgentau; Geh' Geliebter geh' jetzt!

New York 9 April 1958- 9 January 1959	Garvey, piano	LP: Victor LM 2279/LSC 2279 CD: RCA/BMG 09026 614992/09026 681532

RICCARDO ZANDONAI (1883-1944)

Francesca da Rimini, excerpt (Paolo datemi pace!)

Rome 24-28 June 1967	RCA Italiana Orchestra Molinari-Pradelli	LP: Victor LM 2968/LSC 2968/SB 6742 CD: RCA/BMG 09026 612362

TRADITIONAL, MISCELLANEOUS AND SPIRITUALS

Amazing Grace

New York 4-7 April 1966	St.Thomas Choir Self	LP: Victor LM 2918/LSC 2918 CD: RCA/BMG 09026 681532

Angels we have heard on high, arranged by Meyer

Vienna 3-5 June 1961	VPO Karajan	LP: Decca LXT 5657/SXL 2294/JB 38 LP: London 5644/OSA 25280 CD: Decca 421 1032/448 9982

A city called heaven, arranged by Paur

New York 7-18 December 1961	Orchestra Paur	LP: Victor LM 2600/LSC 2600 CD: RCA/BMG 09026 681532

Deep river, arranged by Paur

New York 7-18 December 1961	Orchestra and Chorus Paur	LP: Victor LM 2600/LSC 2600 CD: RCA/BMG 09026 681532

Ev'ry time I feel the spirit, arranged by Dawson

New York 19-22 April 1970	Rust College Choir Holmes	LP: Victor LM 3183/LSC 3183 CD: RCA/BMG 09026 681532

Fairest Lord Jesus/Schlesische Volkslieder

New York 4-7 April 1966	St.Thomas Choir Self	LP: Victor LM 2918/LSC 2918 CD: RCA/BMG 09026 681532

God rest ye merry gentlemen, arranged by Meyer

Vienna 3-5 June 1961	Wiener Singverein VPO Karajan	LP: Decca LXT 5657/SXL 2294/JB 38 LP: London 5644/OSA 25280 CD: Decca 421 1032/448 9982

He's got the whole world in his hands, arranged by Bonds

New York 7-18 December 1961	Orchestra Paur	LP: Victor LM 2600/LSC 2600 CD: RCA/BMG 09026 681532

I couldn't hear nobody pray, arranged by Hall Johnson

New York 19-22 April 1970	Walton Rust College Choir Holmes	LP: Victor LM 3183/LSC 3183 CD: RCA/BMG 09026 681532

I wonder as I wander, arranged by Hayman

New York 21 May 1969	Orchestra Fiedler	LP: Victor PRS 288 CD: RCA/BMG 09026 681532

My way is cloudy, arranged by Hall

New York 19-22 April 1970	Rust College Choir Holmes	LP: Victor LM 3183/LSC 3183 CD: RCA/BMG 09026 681532

Nobody knows the trouble I've seen, arranged by Hall

New York 19-22 April 1970	Rust College Choir Holmes	LP: Victor LM 3183/LSC 3183 CD: RCA/BMG 09026 681532

O Tannenbaum, arranged by Meyer

Vienna 3-5 June 1961	Wiener Singverein VPO Karajan	LP: Decca LXT 5657/SXL 2294/JB 38 LP: London 5644/OSA 25280 CD: Decca 421 1032/448 9982

Sinner please don't let this harvest pass, arranged by Bonds

New York 19-22 April 1970	Rust College Choir Holmes	LP: Victor LM 3183/LSC 3183 CD: RCA/BMG 09026 681532

Sit down servant!

New York 7-18 December 1961	Orchestra and Chorus Paur	LP: Victor LM 2600/LSC 2600 CD: RCA/BMG 09026 681532

Sweet li'l Jesus boy, unaccompanied spiritual arranged by MacGimsey

Vienna 3-5 June 1961		LP: Decca LXT 5657/SXL 2294/JB 38/GRV 10 LP: London 5644/OSA 25280 CD: Decca 421 1032/440 4022/ 440 6542/448 9982
New York 19-22 April 1970		LP: Victor LM 3183/LSC 3183 CD: RCA/BMG 09026 681532

Swing low sweet chariot, arranged by Paur

New York 7-18 December 1961	Orchestra and Chorus Paur	LP: Victor LM 2600/LSC 2600 CD: RCA/BMG 09026 681522/09026 681532

There is a balm in Gilead, arranged by Dawson

New York 19-22 April 1970	Rust College Choir Holmes	LP: Victor LM 3183/LSC 3183 CD: RCA/BMG 09026 681532

This little light of mine, arranged by Bonds

New York 26 January 1991	Garvey, piano	CD: RCA/BMG 09026 681532/09026 684352

Were you there when they crucified my Lord?, unaccompanied spiritual

New York 7-18 December 1961		LP: Victor LM 2600/LSC 2600 CD: RCA/BMG 09026 681532

LEONTYNE PRICE IN INTERVIEW WITH JOHN PFEIFFER

New York
April
1995

CD: RCA/BMG 09026 681532

Credits

Valuable help with the supply of information or illustration material for these discographies came from

Stathis Arfanis, Athens
Christopher Dyment, Welwyn
Richard Chlupaty, London
Clifford Elkin, Glasgow
Bill Flowers, London
Michael Gray, Alexandria VA
Syd Gray, Hove
Bill Holland, Polygram London
Ken Jagger, EMI Classics London
Raymond Klumper-Horneman, London
Roderick Krüsemann, Amsterdam
Johan Maarsingh, Utrecht
Nico Steffen, Huizen
Ronald Taylor, Barnet
Malcolm Walker, Harrow

Discographies by Travis & Emery:

Discographies by John Hunt.

1987: 978-1-906857-14-1: From Adam to Webern: the Recordings of von Karajan.
1991: 978-0-951026-83-0: 3 Italian Conductors and 7 Viennese Sopranos: 10 Discographies: Arturo Toscanini, Guido Cantelli, Carlo Maria Giulini, Elisabeth Schwarzkopf, Irmgard Seefried, Elisabeth Gruemmer, Sena Jurinac, Hilde Gueden, Lisa Della Casa, Rita Streich.
1992: 978-0-951026-85-4: Mid-Century Conductors and More Viennese Singers: 10 Discographies: Karl Boehm, Victor De Sabata, Hans Knappertsbusch, Tullio Serafin, Clemens Krauss, Anton Dermota, Leonie Rysanek, Eberhard Waechter, Maria Reining, Erich Kunz.
1993: 978-0-951026-87-8: More 20th Century Conductors: 7 Discographies: Eugen Jochum, Ferenc Fricsay, Carl Schuricht, Felix Weingartner, Josef Krips, Otto Klemperer, Erich Kleiber.
1994: 978-0-951026-88-5: Giants of the Keyboard: 6 Discographies: Wilhelm Kempff, Walter Gieseking, Edwin Fischer, Clara Haskil, Wilhelm Backhaus, Artur Schnabel.
1994: 978-0-951026-89-2: Six Wagnerian Sopranos: 6 Discographies: Frieda Leider, Kirsten Flagstad, Astrid Varnay, Martha Moedl, Birgit Nilsson, Gwyneth Jones.
1995: 978-0-952582-70-0: Musical Knights: 6 Discographies: Henry Wood, Thomas Beecham, Adrian Boult, John Barbirolli, Reginald Goodall, Malcolm Sargent.
1995: 978-0-952582-71-7: A Notable Quartet: 4 Discographies: Gundula Janowitz, Christa Ludwig, Nicolai Gedda, Dietrich Fischer-Dieskau.
1996: 978-0-952582-72-4: The Post-War German Tradition: 5 Discographies: Rudolf Kempe, Joseph Keilberth, Wolfgang Sawallisch, Rafael Kubelik, Andre Cluytens.
1996: 978-0-952582-73-1: Teachers and Pupils: 7 Discographies: Elisabeth Schwarzkopf, Maria Ivoguen, Maria Cebotari, Meta Seinemeyer, Ljuba Welitsch, Rita Streich, Erna Berger.
1996: 978-0-952582-77-9: Tenors in a Lyric Tradition: 3 Discographies: Peter Anders, Walther Ludwig, Fritz Wunderlich.
1997: 978-0-952582-78-6: The Lyric Baritone: 5 Discographies: Hans Reinmar, Gerhard Huesch, Josef Metternich, Hermann Uhde, Eberhard Waechter.
1997: 978-0-952582-79-3: Hungarians in Exile: 3 Discographies: Fritz Reiner, Antal Dorati, George Szell.
1997: 978-1-901395-00-6: The Art of the Diva: 3 Discographies: Claudia Muzio, Maria Callas, Magda Olivero.
1997: 978-1-901395-01-3: Metropolitan Sopranos: 4 Discographies: Rosa Ponselle, Eleanor Steber, Zinka Milanov, Leontyne Price.
1997: 978-1-901395-02-0: Back From The Shadows: 4 Discographies: Willem Mengelberg, Dimitri Mitropoulos, Hermann Abendroth, Eduard Van Beinum.
1997: 978-1-901395-03-7: More Musical Knights: 4 Discographies: Hamilton Harty, Charles Mackerras, Simon Rattle, John Pritchard.
1998: 978-1-901395-94-5: Conductors On The Yellow Label: 8 Discographies: Fritz Lehmann, Ferdinand Leitner, Ferenc Fricsay, Eugen Jochum, Leopold Ludwig, Artur Rother, Franz Konwitschny, Igor Markevitch.
1998: 978-1-901395-95-2: More Giants of the Keyboard: 5 Discographies: Claudio Arrau, Gyorgy Cziffra, Vladimir Horowitz, Dinu Lipatti, Artur Rubinstein.
1998: 978-1-901395-96-9: Mezzo and Contraltos: 5 Discographies: Janet Baker, Margarete Klose, Kathleen Ferrier, Giulietta Simionato, Elisabeth Hoengen.

1999: 978-1-901395-97-6: The Furtwaengler Sound Sixth Edition: Discography and Concert Listing.
1999: 978-1-901395-98-3: The Great Dictators: 3 Discographies: Evgeny Mravinsky, Artur Rodzinski, Sergiu Celibidache.
1999: 978-1-901395-99-0: Sviatoslav Richter: Pianist of the Century: Discography.
2000: 978-1-901395-04-4: Philharmonic Autocrat 1: Discography of: Herbert Von Karajan [Third Edition].
2000: 978-1-901395-05-1: Wiener Philharmoniker 1 - Vienna Philharmonic and Vienna State Opera Orchestras: Discography Part 1 1905-1954.
2000: 978-1-901395-06-8: Wiener Philharmoniker 2 - Vienna Philharmonic and Vienna State Opera Orchestras: Discography Part 2 1954-1989.
2001: 978-1-901395-07-5: Gramophone Stalwarts: 3 Separate Discographies: Bruno Walter, Erich Leinsdorf, Georg Solti.
2001: 978-1-901395-08-2: Singers of the Third Reich: 5 Discographies: Helge Roswaenge, Tiana Lemnitz, Franz Voelker, Maria Mueller, Max Lorenz.
2001: 978-1-901395-09-9: Philharmonic Autocrat 2: Concert Register of Herbert Von Karajan Second Edition.
2002: 978-1-901395-10-5: Sächsische Staatskapelle Dresden: Complete Discography.
2002: 978-1-901395-11-2: Carlo Maria Giulini: Discography and Concert Register.
2002: 978-1-901395-12-9: Pianists For The Connoisseur: 6 Discographies: Arturo Benedetti Michelangeli, Alfred Cortot, Alexis Weissenberg, Clifford Curzon, Solomon, Elly Ney.
2003: 978-1-901395-14-3: Singers on the Yellow Label: 7 Discographies: Maria Stader, Elfriede Troetschel, Annelies Kupper, Wolfgang Windgassen, Ernst Haefliger, Josef Greindl, Kim Borg.
2003: 978-1-901395-15-0: A Gallic Trio: 3 Discographies: Charles Muench, Paul Paray, Pierre Monteux.
2004: 978-1-901395-16-7: Antal Dorati 1906-1988: Discography and Concert Register.
2004: 978-1-901395-17-4: Columbia 33CX Label Discography.
2004: 978-1-901395-18-1: Great Violinists: 3 Discographies: David Oistrakh, Wolfgang Schneiderhan, Arthur Grumiaux.
2006: 978-1-901395-19-8: Leopold Stokowski: Second Edition of the Discography.
2006: 978-1-901395-20-4: Wagner Im Festspielhaus: Discography of the Bayreuth Festival.
2006: 978-1-901395-21-1: Her Master's Voice: Concert Register and Discography of Dame Elisabeth Schwarzkopf [Third Edition].
2007: 978-1-901395-22-8: Hans Knappertsbusch: Kna: Concert Register and Discography of Hans Knappertsbusch, 1888-1965. Second Edition.
2008: 978-1-901395-23-5: Philips Minigroove: Second Extended Version of the European Discography.
2009: 978-1-901395--24-2: American Classics: The Discographies of Leonard Bernstein and Eugene Ormandy.

Discography by Stephen J. Pettitt, edited by John Hunt:

1987: 978-1-906857-16-5: Philharmonia Orchestra: Complete Discography 1945-1987

Available from: Travis & Emery at 17 Cecil Court, London, UK.
(+44) 20 7 240 2129. email on sales@travis-and-emery.com .

Music and Books published by Travis & Emery Music Bookshop:

Mellers, Wilfrid: Caliban Reborn - Renewal in Twentieth Century Music
Mellers, Wilfrid: François Couperin and the French Classical Tradition
Mellers, Wilfrid: Harmonious Meeting
Mellers, Wilfrid: Le Jardin Retrouvé, The Music of Frederic Mompou
Mellers, Wilfrid: Music and Society, England and the European Tradition
Mellers, Wilfrid: Music in a New Found Land: ... ... American Music
Mellers, Wilfrid: Romanticism and the Twentieth Century (from 1800)
Mellers, Wilfrid: The Masks of Orpheus: ...... the Story of European Music.
Mellers, Wilfrid: The Sonata Principle (from c. 1750)
Mellers, Wilfrid: Vaughan Williams and the Vision of Albion
Panchianio, Cattuffio: Rutzvanscad Il Giovine
Pearce, Charles: Sims Reeves, Fifty Years of Music in England.
Playford, John: An Introduction to the Skill of Musick.
Purcell, Henry et al: Harmonia Sacra ... The First Book, (1726)
Purcell, Henry et al: Harmonia Sacra ... Book II (1726)
Quantz, Johann: Versuch einer Anweisung die Flöte traversiere zu spielen.
Rameau, Jean-Philippe: Code de Musique Pratique, ou Methodes.
Rastall, Richard: The Notation of Western Music.
Rimbault, Edward: The Pianoforte, Its Origins, Progress, and Construction.
Rousseau, Jean Jacques: Dictionnaire de Musique
Rubinstein, Anton : Guide to the proper use of the Pianoforte Pedals.
Sainsbury, John S.: Dictionary of Musicians. Vol. 1. (1825). 2 vols.
Simpson, Christopher: A Compendium of Practical Musick in Five Parts
Spohr, Louis: Autobiography
Spohr, Louis: Grand Violin School
Tans'ur, William: A New Musical Grammar; or The Harmonical Spectator
Terry, Charles Sanford: Four-Part Chorals of J.S. Bach. (German & English)
Terry, Charles Sanford: Joh. Seb. Bach, Cantata Texts, Sacred and Secular.
Terry, Charles Sanford: The Origins of the Family of Bach Musicians.
Tosi, Pierfrancesco: Opinioni de' Cantori Antichi, e Moderni
Van der Straeten, Edmund: History of the Violoncello, The Viol da Gamba ...
Van der Straeten, Edmund: History of the Violin, Its Ancestors... (2 vols.)
Walther, J. G.: Musicalisches Lexikon ober Musicalische Bibliothec

Travis & Emery Music Bookshop
17 Cecil Court, London, WC2N 4EZ, United Kingdom.
Tel. (+44) 20 7240 2129

CPSIA information can be obtained at www.ICGtesting.com
Printed in the USA
244782LV00002B/16/P

9 781901 395013